AF258272

OBSERVATIONS

SUR

L'ÉTAT POLITIQUE

DES

HOMMES DE COULEUR

DE LA GUIANE FRANÇAISE.

Par J.-J. Le Blond,

HABITANT, PROPRIÉTAIRE, CRÉOLE DE CAYENNE.

> Les Rois qu'on trompe de près, on les trompe encore
> mieux de loin ; il est aisé d'en obtenir par le mensonge
> et la surprise des ordres dont ils frémiraient s'ils en
> prévoyaient les abus. MARMONTEL.

NANTES.

IMPRIMERIE DE W. BUSSEUIL ET COMP.

—

30 Avril 1832.

TABLE OF CONTENTS

DEDICATION

This love story is dedicated to the phenomenal women I know and love, and those I haven't yet had the privilege of meeting. I raise my glass in acknowledgment of our shared imperfections, unwavering tenacity, and graceful grit under fire. If it weren't for the women in my life who have kept my lantern aglow, this story of love would never have been born.

To Madame Bulette, my sweet guide and muse, thank you for choosing me as an envoy for your legacy of love. Your quiet, spiritual presence gave me vision, strength, and courage.

We are women in time and beyond time, part of this raw, messy, gorgeous work we call life.

Let's weave our way together through this life, hand in hand, heart to heart, mining the vein of gold that is buried in each of us.

"THE THREADS OF TIME,"

Cheryl Roberts Oliver

Dedicated to Julia Harriet

We are the seamstresses, weavers
of the threads of time, our spirit fingers
stitching portals into what has been that is no more,
a different place, a different form.

This life, the last, the next,
entwined with every breath we take,
so full, so frail. Death knots the thread;
birth spins a new design

formed with sacred colors
of the earth, each dusk and dawn,
reflections of the darkest nights,
always with a flaw to let the spirit out

honoring the imperfections
that overlay the course of growth. Untangling
the threads, we cast on dreams, a slipknot to begin,
then we work the yarn of each existence,

entwined with those that came
before and those ahead. We've all been here.
We will return again, traveling a vast expanse,
tethered to the now, always seeking to enfold

and be enfolded in a warm embrace
that will erase our fears and doubts, using
words to calm and comfort when we're lost
only to be found again.

We are the dreamers,
rising to new heights, falling to great depths,
risking loss and pain, knowing that's the price we
pay for trust and faith to be sustained.

We are the seamstresses,
weavers of the threads, casting on,
working every strand with love, forever
roaming, keepers of unending time.

CHAPTER ONE

WHEN LOVE HITS TURBULENCE

"We're all gonna die!"

Red wine spilled across the wrinkled hand of a woman with painted lips and no eyebrows. Across the aisle, two of her companions made fearful screeching noises as our plane shuddered and slammed through channels of turbulence on approach to the Reno airport. I coiled as much as I could into a fetal position, my trembling feet boring into the seat in front of me.

"Julia, breathe, babe. It will be OK. Planes are built for this."

Expletives of every color and form flowed freely from the pit of doom in my stomach. The old ladies were right—we were fucked.

I was too young to die like this, stuffed in a metal can with wings and a gaggle of purple-haired drunks. I didn't trust any of it: the physics of flight, the perilous desert, or that I would live to see another day. Looking at my boyfriend James, you'd never know there was the slightest concern. Eating salted nuts like he was on the carousel at the fair, his nonchalant demeanor further incited my deepening despondency.

"Are you freaking kidding me? This is fucking terrible. Planes aren't made to fly through this kind of hell, James."

Both freshly graduated from college, James and I had left the lushness of the Pacific Northwest to visit my parents in a valley north of Reno. As recent implants to the high desert, my folks held the highest accolades for this land of wall-to-wall sunshine surrounded by endless hills of buried gemstones. But I wasn't so sure. I had heard of this "Biggest Little City" and imagined it to be a sequined hoax, where sweaty old Elvis had crooned to tweaked-out gamblers. It seemed like the sort of America we should try to snuff out like a Marlboro Red, a smoldering mirage that twinkled like embers atop polyester pants.

Big wet tears flowed down my face as I struggled to breathe amid the constant, jolting chaos. James just stared out the window at rows of trailer parks below, separated by islands of half-dead sagebrush. The airport must be nearby, and I pictured us slamming into the runway as an amorphous fireball, nose over tail, like a little kid missing a step and barreling down a flight of stairs.

"Fuck me. Are we almost there? I seriously can't take much more of this." Flickering memories played like an old movie reel on the lids of my squinched eyes: hugging my mom at the bus stop on my way to kindergarten; my first French kiss in the hallway of my childhood home with my basset hound staring up at us; being handed my college diploma standing before thousands of smiling faces. Suddenly, the plane dropped in altitude. It felt as though my body was yanked out of the seat, but the seatbelt held. A sobering truth snatched at me: I was going to die without ever truly being in love with a man.

"We're gettin' really close now. Any minute, we'll be touching down. I can't wait to see how the pilot lands this thing with such a strong headwind."

I couldn't comprehend James's composure. In fact, it pissed me off. Why didn't he care if we lived or died? He didn't seem to feel passionately about anything, including me. All I could think was that every person who died in a plane crash felt like this beforehand, soaring through thoughts of regret and guilt while conversely praying for mercy because, up here, you knew God's reckoning must not be too far away.

Just then, the ballast of the plane licked the ground. For an instant, gravity's presence felt like an affirmation of survival, until we immediately lifted back off the concrete, the plane's wings wobbling, my chest collapsing.

"OH NO, no, no, no… NO, NO, NO!"

James clutched my hand as the engines forcefully geared down, causing the passengers to lunge violently forward. The grinding brakes quickly slowed us down to a sensible speed, and with the plane stabilized, a collective exhalation and inhalation was shared among the crew and passengers alike.

"I need a stiff drink, James, because I'm not at all OK after this. I thought we were total goners."

"I told you we'd be just fine. Planes are built to handle stress. You have to trust things in life a little more, Julia."

I had no patience for a pep talk. I needed to get the fuck off this plane and make a toast of gratitude for not dying today.

As we arrived at the gate, I was noticeably unhinged, but my untethering wasn't only due to the turbulent flight into Reno. A chain reaction had been set off in my heart, having been slammed with the revelation that true love was absent from my life. A different fireball of sorts took hold of my stomach. I couldn't extinguish this feeling of emptiness. Far worse than perishing in a plane crash was dying without ever knowing love.

James and I went straight to the airport cantina past rows of cajoling slot machines. The bartender took one look at me and poured us two double shots of well tequila. We nodded in appreciation and threw them back like Kool-Aid on a hot summer day. The tequila landed cruelly in my soured stomach, but I willed the upset away, thankful for the numbing effect of booze on my shattered nerves.

Visiting the restroom on our way to baggage claim, I splashed water on my face to revive myself before seeing my parents. Sadly, there was no way to make over the specter that I had become while airborne. Emotionally, something had definitely shifted in me during the flight, and if anyone would be the first to notice, it would be my mom.

"Honey, what the hell happened to you? Are you guys OK?" Swooping me into her arms like an abandoned kitten, I reveled in the first moment of comfort since leaving Seattle. Peeling back enough to take me in again, she enfolded me even tighter. "What happened? You look like Casper the ghost."

"Oh, you know, Mom, I just spent the last hour and a half balled up like a baby while the jet stream played ping-pong with our plane."

"Jesus, sweetie, that sounds plain awful. Let's get you guys back to our place. It's going to get better from here. I promise."

Once pleasantly settled at my folks' new place, glasses of wine in hand, I waited for everything to feel like home, but nothing looked familiar. When we gathered at the dinner table to feast, the knots in my stomach were still coiled. Looking directly into my parents' faces for the first time since our arrival, I pictured them 20 years ago, madly in love with each other. My mom was a pinball wizard and had won my dad a beer by earning the highest score on the machine. That was how they met back in 1978, and theirs was the kind of love I longed for.

"So, we set up a little surprise for you guys while you're in town." Mom looked very excited.

Normally, I would have jumped at such a gesture, but after our harrowing flight out of Dante's Inferno, I felt more apprehensive than appreciative.

"We really don't need anything special, Mom. It's just so wonderful to be here with you guys. We've missed you so much."

"Oh, come on. Don't you want to know what we have in store for you?" my mother insisted, looking baffled by my lack of enthusiasm.

James, steamrolling through my hesitation, piped in, "Well, I want to know. Even if Miss Sour Pants isn't game, I'd love to know what's up next for us."

My puckered face tightened even more, which caught Dad's attention. He squinted knowingly.

"Scott and I got you a night up in an old mining town called Virginia City just east of Reno. It was a boomtown during the gold rush days and still has much of the true flavor of the Wild West. We even got you a spooky room in an old haunted hotel."

James lit up, as he had grown up in Texas, where playing "Cowboys and Indians" was considered a core part of how kids practiced healthy terms of endearment.

"Oh, I've heard of Virginia City," James said. "Mark Twain was a reporter for the town's newspaper in the early 1860s. He wrote some great shit about miners, gunslingers, and general tomfoolery."

While my mom was describing the city and hotel, I had unconsciously started rubbing my chin with my left hand, setting off a visual cue of my apprehension. Dad was watching me closely.

"Julia, honey, what's wrong? Did we miss the boat on this? I figured it would be right up your alley given your love of American history and fun places to explore."

"No, it's not that. It's just been such a long day and I'm wiped. I'm sure it will be great."

The truth was, I wasn't sure of anything. I felt like a tumbleweed, tossed by the whim of the wind. I wanted things to be like they had been when my folks lived in Washington, a state with inherent comforts, liberal democrats, and no-smoking policies.

Situated in a barren wasteland, Reno had a harshness that unsettled me. Casinos erected out of sand resembled false idols wearing neon crowns. People planted concrete yards, and the lack of greenery in the suburbs stirred images of destitute farmers staring blankly at fallow fields during the Great Depression.

I wasn't sure I should trust any place where the jokers ran wild. But it wasn't really any of this that mattered…and I knew it. What had me spinning was the lack of confidence felt in my relationship with a man who didn't appear to be in love with anything, including me. Yet here we were on this adventure together, and I was unable to abort this shared mission.

"A good night's sleep will set everything straight," I announced boldly, hoping that I would somehow return to the complacent Julia who had boarded Flight 3707 to Reno from Seattle. The disconcerting spark of realization that had been ignited inside of me made it clear I couldn't resume the illusions of my former naivete.

CHAPTER TWO

WHEN LOVE RETURNS

Parked on a dusty side street in Virginia City, I opened the car door and nearly stepped onto the boot of an open-armed stranger smiling down on me.

"Well, jumpin' Jehoshaphat! If it ain't you back here to see me in the walkin' flesh."

I turned to James, and in a low murmur so I wouldn't be overheard by the bedraggled-looking character, whispered, "James, who the bloody hell is this guy?"

Not to be put off, the man opened his arms and invited me to "Come on and get over here, sweet lil' missy! We got a lot of catchin' up to do."

I would have given almost anything for a means of escape. No part of me trusted weirdos, especially as utterly unhinged as this guy appeared to be.

James, sensing my trepidation, stood up from the driver's side of our car and joined the conversation. "Hello there, sir. We just rolled into town, so you must be mistaking my girlfriend for somebody else."

Less than two minutes into our visit and things had already gone helter-skelter in Virginia City. I was unsure of the appropriate reaction given nothing like this had ever happened to me before. Shutting the passenger door, I reluctantly accepted his waiting embrace.

"You 'member me, don't ya, honey?" he said, showing puzzlement in his eyebrows. "Because I sure know who you be. You're my most darlin' Julia, my Miss Julia Bulette."

I shot James a dumbstruck look. He was standing closer to me by this point, his mouth open in astonishment.

"Wait, what the heck?! How do you know my name?!" I asked, pausing just long enough to step back and take a deep breath. I continued, "My name *is* Julia…Julia Harriet. As James said, we've never been here or even heard of this place before yesterday."

The man chortled as though the joke was definitely on us. "I got a drink waitin' up at the bar. Come along 'n grab a snoot with me."

Was this some Wild West prank my parents were pulling on us? Habitually, I grabbed James's hand, and we trailed after the man, dumbstruck but curious.

After a quick ascent up a steep block, we hit a rickety wooden boardwalk and took a sharp right. Three doors down, a set of broken concrete steps lead into a dank-looking hole-in-the-wall. We entered wide-eyed and took in the sight of hundreds of lacy bras dangling from the chandelier interspersed with dollar bills poked into the crumbling ceiling. This place had stories to tell.

The man's abandoned drink was sitting on the bar, sweating with condensation. He walked up to it then turned back to us. "Name's Red Dog, case you've forgotten. Hold tight, I'll be back in a sec."

Like a rascal elf, he split stage left, leaving us in this dive of a bar. It felt like James and I had fallen into a wormhole leading us back in time to High Noon. Regrettably, we hadn't dressed for lawlessness or a showdown and, instead, looked the part of two rookies from New York City.

I scanned the room. It was all but empty. A younger gentleman sat alone at a table, rolling a smoke and wrestling with the crisp pages of a newspaper. Behind the bar, clad in black leathers and a brimmed Stetson, was the bartender, weighing in at upwards of 250 pounds.

James ordered a well whiskey, and I requested a vodka tonic to demonstrate that this wasn't my first appearance in a rough-and-tumble bar. I pulled a crisp $20 bill from my purse and placed it on the worn wood. The hulking bartender quickly grabbed it, tossing the bill flippantly toward the register, and then proceeded to give us our drinks.

After we finished our two ordinary but expensive beverages, I finally had to say something. "James, there's no way two shitty well drinks can possibly cost so much. Do you think he's trying to rip us off?"

"Oh, I know he is, and there's nothing we can do about it. We should probably just get out of here before something worse happens."

A switch flipped inside of me, unleashing a spitting fury. No man, however ginormous, was going to bamboozle me. Regardless of our city-slicker demeanors, it was time to pull up my sleeves and double down on this challenge. Justice would be served.

"We aren't going anywhere, James. Just watch this."

Pulling my chest up over the bar like a gymnast on the vault, I called out aggressively to the bartender, "Hey there, we'll take another round."

"I wondered what you were gonna do when I snatched your $20. Ha! You both pass. Welcome on in. The name's Brett." He poured us fresh drinks then handed them to us with a $10 bill and some change.

James placed his hand on my shoulder in celebration of a momentary win for the new kids in town. Brett raised his bottle of beer toward us as a subtle but comforting salute of acceptance.

Abruptly, Red Dog stumbled back through the door with another man in tow who was equally juiced. Based on their stumbling gate, it seemed they had taken a shot, or three, somewhere down the street.

"Billy, look who I found down on D Street pretendin' like she ain't ever been to this place before." Red Dog grabbed Billy by the collar of his frayed jacket, pulling him down into my face. "It's Julia. You know sweet Miss Julia, and this here's her guy, Steve. She came back for us, Billy. She came back to give us some more lovin'."

Steve, aka James, shook Billy's leathery hand, and everyone bellied back up to the bar. Looking pensively at the men's faces, I felt an unexplainable candor with these locals, as though it wasn't our first time sitting shoulder to shoulder in a Wild West bar.

"Red Dog," I said, "will you tell me about Julia, this Julia Bulette who you think I am?" I was on my third drink and could feel the alcohol expanding my tolerance for bullshit and tall tales.

"Oh, I'd love to, honey." Red Dog took a quick sip and flapped his arm excitedly. "Brett, Miss Julia needs to hear some goddamn music with my story. Throw some Joplin on the jukebox, would ya, man?"

"Piece of My Heart" came wailing out of the speakers, and Red Dog nodded ardently to the downbeat until he was ready to bang out his narrative.

"Julia, that's you. You mighta' switched up your last name, but the heart's still the same. You're that sweet madame who welcomed all brokenhearted men like me and old Billy here into your arms for comfort and care, offerin' a love that remains even after everythin' else be leavin' a man broken 'n bone dry. A love that never dies. Do you know what I'm sayin' to you, Miss Julia?"

I would be a bald-faced liar if I claimed to comprehend what Red Dog's riddle meant, but his words resonated in my lower ribs like a deep, penetrating side ache. Joplin's guttural cry warped the dry boards tacked loosely to the walls behind me. Like ore from the earth, something was being dug out of my heart that had never before been excavated. It didn't feel relative to who I knew myself to be: the Julia Harriet that lived with a lackluster boyfriend and worked for a shitty newspaper in Seattle. Something raw was being pulled from the catacombs of my very soul. It felt as massive as Joplin's voice ringing in my ears.

Unsettled, I pondered how I, the woman who had never been in love, could somehow resemble anything like Julia Bulette, the woman who had made men feel healed and held in her love.

Red Dog continued, "How I be knowin' you THE Julia is simple. You've gotta light that pulls me outta my own damn darkness. You shine the light back to love, like a mutherfuckin' lighthouse. Right, Bill?"

Billy was sitting beside me cross-eyed drunk. He looked past me as though I were an apparition. Red Dog slowly began to slump forward, catching himself on the edge of the bar as James swooped under his right armpit to keep him from face-planting into the hardwood.

"All right, time for beddy-bye, Red Dog. Billy, you too." Brett grabbed their drinks and wiped their spots clean. "Better be getting your drunk butts home."

I looked over at James, who was still holding up half of Red Dog, and recognized this was our cue to move along as well. Billy exited slick as a sidewinder, but there was no way Red Dog was going anywhere without help.

"Brett, where does Red Dog live?" I asked.

Brett pointed across the street to a whitewashed wood-framed door. "Right over there. It'll be open."

I slid under Red Dog's empty shoulder, and the three of us hobbled out onto the boardwalk. His apartment was the size of a walk-in closet and smelled oddly like shoe polish. Lowering him onto a twin bed, I removed his hat and set it on a bedside table. Like that, he was out cold. I put my hands to his cheeks as I would tucking in a small child and kissed his furrowed brow. When my lips met his face, I knew I had placed this man gently into bed before. He wasn't a stranger to me. Not at all. He was a man I felt I had known from another time.

Upon finally putting my head on the pillow in our haunted hotel room, I looked over at James. Unlike Red Dog, he suddenly seemed unfamiliar, at least to my heart. How could I sleep next to such a stranger? He was the antithesis of the kind of man I yearned for. A fervor had engulfed me. I had to surrender to it, much as a miner slamming pickaxes into the earth seeking a bounty of silver or gold surrenders to the promise of wealth. I wasn't sure where it would take me, but the feeling was such that I could no longer slumber through the dawn of my own awakening.

CHAPTER THREE

WHEN LOVE FIGHTS BACK

My return to the Northwest felt like a swift kick in the pants. I was back at the newspaper Monday morning, sitting at my desk amid a small sea of soft gray cubicles, feeling like a little lost fish. I was grappling with my growing fascination of the former Madame of Virginia City, Julia Bulette, while simultaneously coming to terms with the apathy that my own life resembled here in Seattle.

As a recent college graduate, taking a "real" job at the local newspaper made perfect sense. I dreamed of becoming the next Carl Bernstein, unearthing political scandal and corruption like a gardener with a razor-sharp mattock. Unfortunately, I was planted down in the circulation department with a bunch of nerdy misanthropes, fielding calls from disgruntled customers seeking lengthy explanations about their misplaced papers.

I knew there was a proverbial ladder that all newbie writers had to climb to reach reporter status, but I didn't realize the first rung would be so far down in the muck and mire of meaninglessness. The only writing I had accomplished thus far was developing a brief script offering two potential solutions to the plethora of angry customers: redelivery or reimbursement.

With my supervisor off to a board meeting upstairs, a tryst with Google search felt justified, especially given that I was an underpaid and unappreciated guppy. I started my online affair by searching for famous quotes from great journalists. At the top of the feed was a link to popular sayings attributed to Mark Twain.

Substitute "damn" every time you're inclined to write "very;" your editor will delete it and the writing will be just as it should be.

I smiled. His humor held such simple, bold truths. I made a mental note about proper adverb usage and dug deeper into this treasure trove of journalistic wisdom.

Realizing I didn't know much about Twain's career in writing, I took a quick peruse of a basic biography that included a timeline of his life. I stopped abruptly upon reading the following passage in an article on History.com:

In need of money, he accepted a job as reporter for a Virginia City, Nevada, newspaper called the *Territorial Enterprise*. His articles covering the bustling frontier-mining town began to appear...in [July]

1862. Like many newspapermen of the day, Clemens adopted a pen name, signing his articles with the name Mark Twain, a term from his old river boating days.

Somehow, all roads were leading my mind and heart straight back to Virginia City. I peered over the crown of my computer to make sure no one had observed my digression into cyber sleuthing then carried on.

It was such an unlikely coincidence that in the place where Clemens adopted his famous moniker, I had also gathered new meaning in my own name. But there was simply no explaining why upon my arrival to town a long-bearded derelict had started hollering at me as if I were his familiar and favorite harlot. That was still beyond me.

Speaking of that, it was time to figure out who the heck Madame Bulette really was. As Red Dog had espoused, she was well loved, but why? What did she know about love that created such sweeping adoration? I wondered if Twain had interviewed Bulette or, better still, if Twain had been a client of the madame.

This was the kind of life I wanted to live. Juicy and full of wonder. Having more questions than answers, I literally said "Damn" aloud as the phone at my desk started ringing. "Hello, this is Julia speaking. How may I help you today?"

"The pimple-nosed twerp who delivers our newspaper keeps tossing it into our juniper bush. Now, how the hell do you expect an 84-year-old veteran to go on diving into a prickly ass shrub to retrieve his paper that he paid his hard-earned money for?"

"I'm truly sorry to hear this, sir. How many papers do you want to be replaced or receive reimbursement for?" I was still scanning the article titles about Bulette that filled the screen while trying to sound sympathetic to this customer's plight.

"I want a whole goddamn year free. That's reasonable for the pain and suffering of this true inconvenience. Your paper isn't worth much these days anyhow with all the pinko reporters you've got dishing up the news."

"I understand. I can pass your request on to my supervisor if you would like."

"I'm guessing that's because you don't have any say in this place, do you, kid? That's the problem these days—everyone's lost their balls and wants someone else to go out and find them."

The man gave me his name, digits, and a visceral threat that he would be walking into the office the following morning if my supervisor didn't return the call.

Upon exiting this curt encounter, I took a sip of cold coffee with scummy cream. The customer was always right—at least, that's what I was told during my two-hour orientation to the newspaper complaint department. Maybe the pricks did have their place as the gatekeepers of veracity, and in all honesty, this old grouch was on to something.

Twain would have certainly kicked dirt onto the typeface of this bullshit place that I called my place of employment, founded on regimen and misery. Real news was made by risk-takers, inventors, and magicians. If I were ever going to find true love, I couldn't work in a place that avoided stories of passion and wonder to appease the mediocrity of America. I had to summon my inner cojones and allow the feelings aroused in Virginia City to consume me whole.

CHAPTER FOUR

WHEN LOVE BREAKS

Genitals. Second only to the word *pubic* in the lexicon of crushingly awful terms uttered within a sexual education curriculum. My high school health teacher wore purple sweatpants outfits and definitely wasn't getting laid. But she took maniacal pleasure from the role of coital gatekeeper and instructed us in a way that extracted all the connection out of copulation, leaving behind only a penis, a vagina, and trepidation.

At age 23, I'd had sex with only two men—Jeff being one and James being the other—and I had never made love with either of them. Lovemaking required the feeling of being in love, or so I imagined, which remained elusive to me. I definitely needed real guidance and direction when it came to intimacy in the bedroom, so the decision to choose Julia Bulette as my new madame mentor was a no-brainer.

Up to this point, intercourse seemed more about giving in and giving over than it did about making meaningful connections. Honestly, my first two boyfriends would have been better kept in the friend zone. The transition to becoming sexual partners was more a reflection of their desire for fornication than it was of developing deeper intimacy. I wanted to be touched by someone and feel something more than pure physical stimulation. There had to be more to sex than just getting off...I hoped.

My first question for Bulette was simple: Do you have to be in love to make love?

Sandwiched between two flimsy walls of a cubicle, a numbness enveloped me, a lack of lust that no 23-year-old should own. I had to act quickly before I became an angry middle-aged housewife living vicariously through soap opera affairs. I had already settled into playing a passive partner to James, a guy who never felt anything resembling passion. We were just two kids limping along in a fashion that would make our grandparents yawn.

Secretly, I coveted a fictional love story, constructed out of fairy tales and dramatic TV shows that I had penned when I was thirteen. Like a special locket, I opened the folded-up notebook pages held in my journal pocket for inspiration and a vacation from my own relationship monotony.

In it, I cast myself as a stormy yet affectionately kind femme fatale, just out of reach of every man in hot pursuit. Every man but the one I created. The one with soft green eyes and a whimsical smile who always found me out in the world. Whether it was backstage at a theater or down by the railroad tracks, he was the only man I allowed to kiss me on the lips because that was where real love was made. Where two became one. It was a lovely fantasy I held onto.

One particularly rainy Saturday in Seattle, I opened the pages of my love story and dabbled with the plot twist of turning my character into a high-brow prostitute. Because of having Bulette's biography intertwined with my imagination, it was easy to picture the scene, the game, and the audacious lifestyle. In my daydream, I was a woman who owned the power between her thighs and knew how to command a man's lust by the simple turn of my head. There was certainly nothing trashy or demeaning about that. In fact, I couldn't help but smile.

I wanted to blame the men I had taken up with for my current dispassion, but I knew that the key to unlocking true love would not be achieved by acquiring the right locksmith. It required the removal of the lock altogether.

Bulette had chucked the societal standards and norms of the 1860s out the window at a time when women were treated as property by men. Traveling from New Orleans to Virginia City, she opened and ran her own profitable business, gave generously to community charities, and fundraised passionately for the local fire department, all while rooted firmly in her sexuality.

Whatever had shaken loose in my heart some seven hundred miles away from Seattle, in an old mining town, was desperate to root itself in my life now. A formidable beckoning called out to me. I wanted to take command of my femininity, to grab my crotch and scream like Kali that I was Woman, and I'm coming for you.

My comeback tour popped off with picking a new man to come with me. I opted for a musician. A brokenhearted lyricist. Someone lacking predictability or permanence. His name was Shane. He rented a room in a shared house with an assortment of punk rock lesbians. His space was completely packed with boxes of stacked poetry books and woven blankets. Like all good Bohemians, Shane was broke and needed chauffeuring about town because he only had a bus pass.

There was one thing though: He was always terribly sad. I admired his commitment to feeling something so consistently and profusely. I took Shane out to teriyaki lunches and fucked him in the back seat of my Jeep Cherokee on the outskirts of town. He read me sonnets and I wrote him haikus about the ocean, creating a common vein of reciprocal verbosity between us. When we neared orgasm, he looked me in the eyes with feeling. In his celestial stare, there was an emotional intelligence that made us more than two animals humping. I considered it a marker that I was on the right track to making love.

The thing about foraging through sexual frivolity, it is easy to forgo the cautionary signposts along the way. Now that I had tasted "the feeling," I wanted more and more. I allowed it to overwhelm my sensibilities. Having volunteered at an AIDS clinic for several years in my teens, I was well versed regarding the ins and outs of safe sex practices. But in my quest to feel romance, I rejected all barriers for the sake of responsiveness, and Shane and I never used protection. The inherent risk actually intensified "the feeling," and I started believing I was finally falling in love.

That was, until he told me he was leaving for England to resume things with an old lover with the name of a flower. A few days later, I dropped him off to donate plasma for cash before leaving the country and said goodbye casually on a sidewalk in Seattle. That's when it became a tragic love story: I had a bun in the oven.

Approaching motherhood in this abhorrently haphazard way just didn't make sense. I had wanted to find and make love, not end up a struggling single mom in my early twenties. Both sides of this coin equaled loss. I was mortified that I had loved him with such reckless abandon, throwing aside my own moral and physical codes. I was swallowed whole in the belly of regretful shame. I held myself, hoping to awaken from this nightmare. "The feeling" had led me into an active minefield, and here I was, fully loaded and tiptoeing toward an excruciating choice. Indignity and guilt were putting on a flamboyant show in my heart, and all I could do was watch, holding my hand to my chest in horror as my life imploded.

I knew women had done it since the beginning of time. I wondered what Bulette would say to me and how prostitutes supported each other through unwanted pregnancies during her time. I had never faced such brutal ugliness. Whether or not I morally agreed with abortion was secondary to the fact that I would be making a life-or-death decision. I pictured the protestors outside of Planned Parenthood yelling "murderer" at me. The right to choose was no choice at all. Either way, I was losing. What I needed to do with my own body, for my best interest, was at the cost of another.

No matter what, I couldn't tell anyone, not even a medical professional. I didn't have the courage to say aloud what I had done, nor did I have women like Bulette in my life whom I could confide in. The only way to protect myself was to omit this disaster from my narrative and handle what I had done without help.

Upon conducting some research, there was no good or safe way to do it without a doctor. That said, there were ways. I found an online article that guided me step by step. Alone in my house, silently hating myself as I took command of two fates with a single act: committing sin in the pursuit of lovemaking. I despised "the feeling" that had lured me into this perversion of passion.

Looking in the mirror of my bathroom, I witnessed a villain looking back at me. No one could ever know that I had committed such a crime in the name of trying to find love. I closed the door to my heart, confining any hope of love to the darkness. How could I ever trust "the feeling" again? The answer to my question was brutally clear: love-making was a perilous game best left to the professionals. The pursuit of love had dragged me, as a novice, into the wilds without a map or a partner. I was totally alone and felt this was a well-deserved punishment. A life sentence of singledom or, at least, separation from love's source.

So, I did what any person who is afraid, broken, and suffering does. I gave my notice at the newspaper and ran.

CHAPTER FIVE

WHEN LOVE RUNS

Wild rabbits scamper fast across the desert sand. That's exactly what I had to do. Skedaddle from the troubled waters of the Pacific Northwest to join the 24-hour circus known as Reno, "The Biggest Little City in the World." This boomtown was built on beginner's luck and rampaging flamboyance, both of which tempted my untethered soul. After committing a violation of the most basic ethical code of "do no harm," here I was, seeking asylum in a place that prided itself on cheap booze, open-carry rights, and professional gambling. It felt like a forgiving harbor in which to moor my moral quandaries while I tried to put myself back together.

My parents were happily established in a valley north of the city, and my postcollege meltdown was lighting up their radar. My mom had seen more than just a woman frazzled by a bad flight when James and I had come to visit the year prior. She knew that look of despair shading my eyes gray and phoned me more than normal these days to check in. As a family, we were a tripod of love, laughter, and like-mindedness. The distance between us stoked the desire to geographically reconvene, and this was my chance.

My dad had heard that the Washoe County School District was hiring anyone with a Bachelor of Arts to fill many vacant full-time teaching positions. Was this some twenty-first-century version of a Gold Rush Renaissance, one in which kids like me could flee the fate of a one-track professional life after college for the freedom of choice? Witnessing the "nine-to-five" fates of our parents' work tedium had undoubtedly rubbed off on us and influenced our generation's urgency for this divergence.

Before leaving for Reno, my cubicle clan at the newspaper threw me a Jimmy Buffet-themed going-away party, which was a fitting send-off to a land-locked version of Margaritaville. But there was no easy escape to paradise for my minced-up heart, which held more saturated pain than a greasy cheeseburger. No amount of neon glow could obscure the truth that I felt like the killer as well as the victim of my own crime. Unfortunately, no amount of tequila could wash away the ugliness of that conundrum.

I hit the freeway and headed south the next morning with my car full of vintage shoes, sweatshirts, and self-care products. Singing punk ballads over miles of highway with my bare arm waving out the window, I mined this moment for a vein of redemption. Leaving Susanville, California, I entered the final stretch of barren roadway to my new home. It was hour eleven of the drive, and my eyes struggled to stay focused. The music had played itself out somewhere in the Sierras, and I found myself placed between peaceful rolling sagebrush and the rage of speeding semitrucks.

Then the strangest thing happened. A zephyr wind blew into the car carrying a woman's voice and sang out to me, *"You, you are known here."*

Jolted out of a driving daydream, my eyes darted reactively to the rearview mirror. Who had just spoken to me?

"Hello? Hello?" I shouted to the wind. No, it didn't make sense calling out to the wind or whatever had spoken. Still, I had heard a woman, and her words were directed at me from somewhere, somehow.

"You are known here, Julia. You are home."

My heart jumped up to my teeth as I heard her voice again, speaking to me directly without a face and calling out to me by name. If it had happened once, I could have written it off as merely being road weary. But not twice, unless I was damn punch-drunk. I better get to Reno fast, because either way, I was losing it. Rolling down all the windows, the smell of warm sage at night reassured my shaken nerves. Homesteads speckled in the western hills captured my attention, almost as though I was looking for an old plot of land I once tended. I was no naysayer to magic, but I didn't trust much at this point, and certainly not hitchhiking ghosts in the desert.

I was closing in on Reno, this time without the screaming fear of annihilation that I'd experienced on the plane flying in to visit my parents. This time, I was welcomed by rows of tract houses, strip malls, and blinking billboards. Descending into town from the north made me feel like a marauder storming an unsuspecting camp of settlers. I wasn't sure what there was to plunder, but the glorious array of dancing lights made it feel like I'd discovered El Dorado, the Lost City of Gold.

Before leaving Seattle, I had secured a little rental house downtown, one block off the Truckee River that flowed beautifully out of Lake Tahoe. Built like a dollhouse, it was a perfect place for a small woman who needed close boundaries. For my first night in town, I decided to check out a neighborhood haunt, just a block away, called Brickies Tavern. Heralding its opening in 1956, the place prided itself on being a union-friendly establishment founded on the backs of its staunch locals. As a fresh-faced 24-year-old from out of town, I figured my unexpected entrance would incite attention.

Stepping in, I met a bar overrun with middle-aged men. They all turned toward the door, some with expressions of excitement, others of befuddlement.

"Look, Mike, your birthday-boy dreams have come true!"

The robust group chortled as one man slapped another on the back of his shiny bald head. I assumed that was Mike.

"Hey, honey, come on over here, and we'll introduce you to everyone. We promise we won't bite."

This was quite the juxtaposition from Seattle, notorious for its citywide effect called "the freeze," in which no one makes eye contact or engages in conversation at the bar, not even the bartender. Walking into Brickies felt like rolling into a boisterous family reunion.

"My name's Julia, and I'm your new neighbor from down the street. I'd love to celebrate Mike's birthday with you all."

I asked kindly for a bottle of Sierra Nevada and walked up to a stool freshly exited by one of Mike's buddies. The eagerness held in the smiles of this group warmed my soured heart. There was a wholesome genuineness that bridged the difference in our ages, genders, backgrounds, and beliefs. I felt a sense of instant comradery, at ease with these men dressed in Carhartt jackets and bibbed overalls, their culture visible, their work illustrated as true friendship. The credo, a Mark Twain quote, hanging above the bar stated, "When in doubt, tell the truth."

"So, what drew a young lady like you into an old folks joint like this?"

"Well, I took a teaching job north of town and am looking to make some new friends. I can already tell I've found a great spot right here."

"We normally don't let whippersnappers like you get too comfortable in here because your generation tends to think you know more than us old-timers. But for you, we'll make an exception. We like your style."

"Great, because I don't tend to enjoy the company of people my own age either. I'm here to learn more than I already know. So, tell me about what you all do for a living that puts you in a union bar like this."

Everyone paused to take a drink. Round-robin style, the men took turns sharing stories about their trade. There was an electrician, a welder, a heavy equipment operator, and so on. What surprised me was not what they did but how they spoke of their work. Each man held his own legacy of moving from apprentice to master in his field. They spoke about the trials and tribulations that came with solving real-world problems and puzzles with their own hands.

Mike cleared his throat and spoke to me.

"You know what, Julia? 'Work is love made visible.' That's a quote, by the way. Work is about bringing love into everything you do. Whether you're paving a road or pulling a bad tooth, if you approach the task with love, it works much better for everyone involved. If you want to make a difference in kids' lives as a teacher, do that. The only way you will be successful is if you put love into it."

The combination of my current fragility and the dark beer resulted in warm tears welling up in my eyes as I took in Mike's words.

"Thank you, Mike. That's exactly the type of wisdom that I needed tonight. I'll be back for more because I'm just a kid that doesn't know shit. And boy, do I ever own that as truth. Here's to good friends, good work, and wise old guys."

Bringing the last of my beer to my lips, I sipped on effervescent knowledge, taking it in slowly and with newfound hope. Perhaps the penance for my sins against love wasn't solitary confinement in an emotional Alcatraz. Rather, it was to be surrounded by a bunch of blue-collar 50-year-old guys who worked for love. They had a lot to teach me, and I certainly did have a lot to learn. The bottom line, it was clear I was here for a reason, and all I had to do was keep showing up.

CHAPTER SIX

WHEN LOVE DISGUISES

When you see a man enter a party dressed as Frida Kahlo, it's hard not to turn your head in adoration. It was Halloween, my favorite holiday, and as a fresh implant to Reno, I wanted to bring my A game to the local festivities. A newly made friend had invited me over for a quaint gathering at her house and enticed me with the fact that the "cutest guy in Reno" would be in attendance. She texted me his photo, and it was hard to deny his deliciousness.

Before I knew it, hours had skipped by at the party like the ping-pong balls being served in the drinking game nearby. Somewhere down the slope of my fourth beer, the front door opened and I realized this was the match point. Wrapped in a colorful serape, with a perfectly penciled unibrow, stood the most physically attractive being I had ever encountered.

Brilliantly buzzed and sporting pink bunny ears, I bounced out of my chair to plunk Frida Kahlo into my basket.

"Oh my God, you totally nailed it with this costume. But I've got to paint your nails for you to clinch it."

Recoiling from my uninhibited approach, Frida's hesitancy did nothing to slow my advances. "OK, sure, but can I grab a beer first? The name's Derek, by the way."

Derek. This fantastic man dressed as a woman had a name. Thanks to copious amounts of alcohol and the ruse of Halloween, I had momentarily forgotten that I was heartbroken. But I did know that with every treat came an equal trick. There was no way I would let myself fall prey like Snow White to a second poison apple. With these thoughts swirling through my inebriated mind, my friend magically appeared with a bottle of red fingernail polish and a cold beer for Derek. She shot me a quick wink like a flickering jack-o'-lantern and split, leaving us at the small kitchen table.

"So why Frida?" I asked matter-of-factly while taking his long, calloused fingers into my palm. Unfortunately, red nail polish is woefully unforgiving, and my tipsy line work caused his hands to look like that of an axe murderer rather than a world-renowned artist.

"I'm a muralist and I love Frida's work. I've been studying twentieth-century painters for an upcoming project and have been looking at her husband Diego Rivera's work. And it was a no-brainer to dress up like her because I've got the eyebrows and lips for it."

"You know, Diego was a real dick. A womanizing fat fuck, if you ask me."

Derek hadn't asked me. But he chuckled at my brash and sudden analysis. "Yeah, he was definitely no good to Frida. But the guy made some amazing murals. Not everyone can be good at everything, you know."

Even under a half-drunken spell, I couldn't help but awaken to this truth. Who was I to be throwing darts at a dead guy who sucked at love? At least he put passion into his paintbrush and made love with paint. I screwed the lid back onto the little glass bottle and looked Derek square in the eye.

"I'm going to kiss you now. I hope that's OK." Grabbing his petal-soft cheeks, I came in hard like my time was for hire. A beer bottle cascaded to the carpet as I fully committed, tongue first, to claim my conquest. I imagined Frida rolled over in her grave at this graceless spectacle, while Diego took to the floor laughing hysterically. Upon retreating from his mouth, I caught a look of amusement with a twist of concern on Derek's face. I shot him a cockeyed and uncertain smile in return, as though to say, "I know, I'm a hot mess."

In my next act, I awakened under an itchy blanket on my friend's couch surrounded by empty keg cups, beer bottles, and pizza boxes. The trick, as I expected, was on me as once again I landed on my ass in this cruel comedic tragedy called my life. It made sense why intelligent women swore off love completely because if it didn't kill you, it was at least going to make you out to be a fucking idiot.

Though certainly no walk of shame, the pathway home was riddled with potholes of self-doubt. I sought a simple remedy to my ridiculing thoughts—a hot cup of coffee, hoping molten java would burn away the heartstrings that kept placing me into perpetual embarrassment. Remembering there was a hole-in-the-wall café nearby, I sought out a simple place to digest some comfort and shake off yet another hit to my ego.

Disheveled and sporting a beer-stained pink T-shirt, I looked like any college kid after a weekend bender. To my right, up against a sidebar, perched a mysterious gentleman with a long, gaunt face accentuated by a black Stetson worn atop his sizable head. His bristly white beard landed just above a polished silver belt buckle. Next to his breakfast plate sat an open three-ring binder filled with photos cased in clear plastic. Organized on an open page were silhouettes of attractive-looking women adorned in various and sundry sparkly metallics and gemstones.

"Good morning, wild-looking woman. Fortunately, you've landed in the right place to sew yourself back together."

I nodded at the man, squinching my cheeks in resentful acknowledgment. After struggling to order a coffee and bagel, I turned to find the man still waiting, clearly anticipating a conversation. Sodden anonymity was not in the cards.

"Young lady, do you have a minute so I could show you something?"

I might be young, but I was old enough to know that when a man, a stranger nonetheless, offers to "show you something," it was a sign to become alarmed. But in his well-meaning smile, there was depth that made me pause just long enough to return curiosity. I did, however, make sure the barista was watching just in case I had to holler for backup.

"All right. OK, I'll bite. What's your name and what's up with this binder of yours?"

"Name is Larry. I'm a silversmith up in a place called Virginia City. Want to see some of my artwork? I think you're going to really dig it."

Of course Larry was from Virginia City, and here he was with a notebook of barely dressed and highly adorned women. Why not? It seemed like Halloween wasn't over just yet.

"Yes, yes, I do actually want to see your work, Larry. My name's Julia Harriet. Please, tell me what you do."

Larry took me through pages of young women ornamented in jewelry reminiscent of that donned by Egyptian goddesses. Hidden in this raggedy man was a fine artist and a silversmith to boot.

"Jesus, you have an incredible talent, Larry. Each piece holds so much unique character. I've never seen anything like your creations."

"Julia, I think you would be a perfect model for my jewelry. Are you interested in coming to my studio and trying on some pieces?"

Here I was, being offered a modeling gig while looking like I fell from the balcony of a frat house. Bemused, I couldn't resist the allure of becoming one of the adorned goddesses too.

He added, "I'll make a nice dinner for us, and afterward, we can do the photo shoot. It will be fun."

Dinner, huh? That didn't seem the slightest bit professional, but I figured all models had to schmooze with their handlers, so I wrote it off as part of navigating the industry standard.

After we agreed on a date and time, I took his business card and walked back to my car.

Settling into the driver's seat, I shut my eyes. Although I didn't know what the hell I was doing, I recognized that synchronicity was brewing in these chance meetings and random conversations. I knew intuitively that they were taking me to a greater place than my life had previously known. I felt as though I was being asked to stop trying so hard and to allow myself to be guided by this unseen force. Could this be the work of the woman who called out to me the night I drove into town? I had to find out who she was and why she wanted me here. Opening my eyes again, I knew I had to start listening to the very thing I had put to sleep—my heart.

CHAPTER SEVEN

WHEN LOVE COMES TO DINNER

If there was ever a road to make your asshole pucker, it's the Old Geiger Grade from Reno to Virginia City. Originally constructed in 1862 as a thoroughfare to move millions of dollars in silver mined from the Comstock Lode down to the Truckee Meadows, it was a highway of reckoning, with harrowing markers such as Dead Man's Point and Robber's Roost. With a 1,700-foot elevation gain, even the modern version of this highway resembled a haphazardly built playground occasionally sprinkled in shards of loose red rock that spilled off the hillside without warning.

Like a 20-something wannabe model, I dressed to impress and packed a ten-dollar bottle of wine, which was quite an upgrade from my usual two-buck plonk. As I wound my way up to Larry's house, I imagined stagecoaches barreling around the hairpin corners, with horses pounding the dry dirt with tenacity.

Larry's home was crafted of the same rusty rock that I had carefully avoided hitting on the road up from Reno. As I stepped out of my car, Larry appeared from a weathered basement door. His round spectacles caught the warm glow of the late summer's evening, casting a friendly twinkle back in my direction.

"Welcome, dear Julia, welcome. Welcome to my humble abode that's also known as my Mad Hatter's Studio."

Larry wasn't kidding. Every inch of his house was covered in doodads, trinkets, tools, jewels, and ancient-looking statuettes. He poured us both a glass of wine and pulled out a rickety wooden chair from his kitchen table with a stack of dusty books piled on the seat. Larry threw them on the floor next to a stack of dusty *Life* magazines from the 1970s, and we took a simultaneous sip to settle in.

"Sorry the place is a bit of a nightmare. Since my wife's passing, I haven't kept up with the housekeeping."

"Your collections are really cool, Larry, so it's no worry to me. And I'm very sorry to hear about your wife. How long has she been gone?"

"Over two years now. She had cancer twice. Beat it the first time but lost round two." His eyes were pools of glacier water, then they filled with warmth. "Julia, have you ever encountered someone so fantastic, almost angelic in profound beauty, that they altered your entire existence?

That's what my wife Mary did to me. She came into my life, which was a pretty good life, and breathed love into my whole being. I had never really known how to breathe until she showed me with her sweet lips."

The pungent scent of envy with a twist of total ignorance rose from my gut to my tongue. What Larry described with his wife was nothing I could relate to or even comprehend. I wanted to experience a love like that so badly, but the more I desired it, the faster it turned back around to bite me.

"No, I've never experienced anything close to that, Larry. But I want it more than I've ever wanted anything. To love and be loved as though you are breathing from the same set of lungs. I went after love once and it stung me hard. I'm still digesting its poisonous effects. I'm not sure I could live through something like that again."

"You can't quit love, Julia. Even if your heart is sick from it right now, or you think it would be better to somehow swear off love, love doesn't stop just because you give up. It's like gravity. Whether you believe in it or not, it's going to be there, and it will influence everything you do. People who resist that kind of truth end up in a bad way, far worse than the painful sting you might be feeling now."

I took wine into my mouth like I was rinsing off the scum of my past relationships. Larry was right. Beyond right or wrong, he had just told me something that I could not deny or avoid. Running from love wasn't working. Chasing after it wasn't working either.

"Thank you, Larry. Your words touch me deeply even if I don't understand the 'how' in this thing called 'loving' just yet."

He stood up contently, knowing that he had just extended me a priceless nugget of relationship gold. Approaching the sink, he lifted a baking dish containing a whole chicken with cut-up vegetables and placed it in the oven.

"Let's go down to the studio while dinner cooks, and I can show you my latest collection of jewelry. You can pick out which ones you want to model, and we'll do the photo shoot after we eat. Sound like a plan?"

"Absolutely. I can't wait to see your actual work, not to mention your Mad Hatter's Studio."

We carefully stepped down a small flight of stairs littered with vintage shoes and antique books until we entered a large open room with a rectangular worktable in the center. On it were ornate tools and black velvet trays holding hundreds of intricate silver creations.

"Wow, Larry. These are stunning. May I touch them? How long have you been making pieces like this?"

"Since I was a kid. I collected beads and charms that my dad brought me from his travels around the world. When I was in my early twenties, I decided to open a trading company in Carson City, which became a successful bead emporium. One day a man came into the shop who was a silversmith. We really hit it off, and he offered to take me under his wing. The guy was a master. I'm still just learning the trade, but I've been making my jewelry ever since."

I watched Larry pick up an agate pendant shaped like a dragonfly. He grinned as he cradled it with the care of a man who had breathed life into its wings.

"This one is for you. The dragonfly symbolizes living without regret and moving swiftly from the past to the present moment. Please, take this home with you. All I ask is that you let me snap a photo of you wearing it before you leave to add to my book."

"Oh my goodness, Larry. I'm speechless. I adore dragonflies. To me, they are pure magic. I will treasure it."

"Let the dragonfly remind you that someday—maybe tomorrow, maybe years from now—a man will fly into your heart with ease and grace and bring you joy. Love takes work to maintain, but with the right initial spark, the work will bring you endless happiness."

Larry and I returned to the kitchen, refilling our empty glasses. He checked on the chicken. The bird was definitely baked. I had a strange moment, thinking, "No one's goose is cooked" and recalled the warning from my friends back at Brickies Tavern to stay away from strange guys who bring books of half-naked women into cafés for show-and-tell. I figured in truth that they were probably a little jealous that I was hanging out with a new old guy outside of them.

"So, Julia," he said, putting our food on the table, "has a man ever made you see stars by what he can do with his tongue in between your legs?"

Whoa, Nellie! I didn't want my friends' warnings to hit home so quickly. I thought Larry and I were exploring territory that could draw us into the land of sensuality, but dammit, I didn't peg him to be some jeweler pervert preying on young women with his artistic allure and talk of love.

"I'm no rookie to what a good lover is, Larry."

"I'm asking you because that's my specialty." He took a mouthful of chicken and chewed with his mouth slightly ajar while looking me in the eyes.

I contemplated throwing my plate of food on the ground and storming out, as this divergence south felt like a breach of trust. But something told me to hold fast.

"Look, I want to be clear that I didn't come here to have sex with you. I'm here because I wanted to see your jewelry and maybe end up the next beautiful model in your book. But if I have to screw you to do that, then I'll leave now."

He dropped his fork onto his plate and his face fell forward. "Oh, Jesus. I'm truly so sorry, Julia. It wasn't my intention to make you feel awkward or upset by asking. And clearly, I did. I get so lonely sometimes living here by myself that I get all tangled up in my thoughts and wishes. I just miss the intimacy. The experience of making love and being touched by love. But that's no excuse if I creeped you out. My apologies, again."

"Understood, Larry." I didn't entirely; however, his apology was enough to settle my hackles. I knew he wasn't intentionally fucking with me, but I also felt inclined to finish my meal quickly and mosey along. "I'm OK if we take a couple of photos of me in the dragonfly piece, and afterward, I'll make my way back home. Deal?"

It felt like a generous deal, one my buddies would have surely booed at, but I was going to play this out my way. Before going back downstairs, I discretely swiped my pocketknife from my purse to avoid the possibility of being the next face on a missing person's flyer in Reno.

"Thank you for hearing me out," he said. "Please take and enjoy the dragonfly. It belongs with you."

"I appreciate the dinner and conversation, Larry, not to mention the gift of this dragonfly and what it symbolizes."

"You're most welcome. I will email the photos once I edit them. And one last thing: To quote the Mad Hatter, 'the secret is to surround yourself with people who make your heart smile. It's then, only then, that you'll find Wonderland.' Whatever you do, Julia, never stop believing you will find the one who breathes life into you. You just have to stop chasing after him so he can come to you."

CHAPTER EIGHT

WHEN LOVE LEARNS

"Ms. Anderson, Eddie forgot his shoes again and his feet look like yucky old eggplants!"

I peered up the school bus steps and saw the small boy with naked, pruned-up feet that did indeed resemble angry produce. Fuck, how the hell did a 10-year-old kid end up at school like this on a snowy day with no shoes?

I had assumed upon accepting the position of Special Education Teacher in a Title I school that I would be properly trained to meet the needs of my learners. They knew I had never worked with kids back in Seattle, let alone children with life-threatening conditions and disabilities. Much to my dismay, when I arrived to begin my first day of teaching, I was simply handed a lanyard with my name on it, told to get my kids off the bus, and provided with the class list of names. It felt like nothing short of landing in the jungles of

Vietnam, being tossed an M-16 rifle, and told, "Good luck, mofo."

Fortunately, I was blessed with a solid sense of humor. I was also paired with a seasoned mentor who took my quivering hand firmly but gently into the school. Miss Darlene had the stature of a Greek goddess and an attitude of a smoking gun. She told me about her five audacious daughters and how she mesmerized the most ill-behaved kids with her dark chocolate voice, her infectious laugh, and rings that blinged atop every finger.

It was the day that Eddie showed up at school without shoes that awakened me to the amount of raw pain on this planet. I couldn't comprehend how a precious and vulnerable child with a developmental disability could be left to fend off the harsh desert terrain on his own. I boldly asked Darlene, "What the hell is wrong with this world, and how can I rescue children like Eddie who are barely making it?"

"Honey," Darlene said when she saw how upset I was, "let's take a little break and step outside. I know it's cold, but it'll do your mind and heart some good."

Darlene was right. I needed to cool off, which was unavoidable as winter's wind licked into the hollows of my ears.

"Julia, here's the thing, sweetie: You're only job at this school is to show up and love these kids. Do you understand what I'm saying? Because that's the most important thing you can do if you want to change these kids' lives. Love each one as your very own. When they're in your classroom, show them the kind of love that can pierce through all the bullshit they see at home. That's how you can make a difference."

Tears streamed down my cheeks, becoming icicles on my chin. "But isn't there something more I can do to help kids like Eddie not have to live like this?"

Darlene inhaled deeply from the long cigarette between her frozen fingers.

"Listen again to me, sweetheart: You just love them. You don't try to rescue them or make them ever think that you could. Because you can't. Make each one of them feel like the most important person on the planet. That their voice matters. That they can believe in magic and that they are magic. Do that, Julia. Every single damn day the kids come to your classroom. And if you do, each one of them will do better out there in the world because you will have taught them love, and they will carry that love with them wherever they go."

I heard the bell ring, and I threw myself into Darlene's arms, overwhelmed with gratitude.

"OK, Darlene. I can do this. I will love the kids in my class more than I've ever loved anything. I've got this."

The following week was Thanksgiving break. I had extended family visiting from Seattle and thought it would be fun to show them a taste of the nightlife in downtown Reno. It was time to bury the knowledge that many of my students would be at home without parents, nourishment, or comfort.

We wandered into the Silver Legacy, my favorite gambling establishment. The owners had sprinkled enough glitter to coat the ominous sense of demise and gluttony generally felt in casinos. As a teacher, I was predictably broke. But I had $20 cash in my purse for one purpose only: to win the kids' Christmas.

My students were fourth through sixth graders, but many were developmentally closer to the mindset and behavior of a three-year-old. Every one of them believed wholeheartedly in Santa. But only five of the fourteen kids had experienced Christmas morning with Santa bringing them a present. As a privileged white woman from the Seattle area, this blew my fucking mind. I couldn't imagine it. How could the kids make sense of holding a belief in something that never came true?

Inspired by the call to love that Darlene instilled in me, I sat my ass down at the Wheel of Fortune slot machine and slid my whole twenty-dollar bill in. Holding a gin and tonic in my left hand and the arm of the machine in my right, I was going to save Christmas. I had to win enough to buy fourteen kids a special present, and I figured I needed about $400.

"Wheel, I need your help. I've got a class of kids who deserve to have their dreams come true. Help me be their elf today. Help me show them that love wins. No matter what." I pulled that lever like I was opening the door to one of the great pyramids. Three cherries lit up the screen, and I was up $100.

"Thank you! Thank you, dear Wheel, but I need a little more of your help. You see, Rochelle wants a pretty doll, and Eddie wants a set of hot wheels."

I took the arm again and shut my eyes. The feeling of love overtook my whole body. I pictured the faces of each child in my class and wrapped them in this feeling. It was different from any sexual or romantic feeling I'd ever had. This was something almighty and magical. This was a kind of love that was pure, a force as strong as…gravity!

I released the lever, and what I saw on the slot machine screen was like seeing Santa appear before me himself.

"Jackpot! Holy cow! I did it! I fucking made Christmas! I did it, kids, I did it! I love you so much!" I bowed reverently to the Great Wheel and cashed out my bonanza.

Seeing my excitement, an older gentleman came over and touched my shoulder. He said, "I heard you talking to that machine about love and making magic happen. You did it, kid. You made the Wheel turn in your favor."

I hugged him as if I had just won the Price is Right then ran over to my relatives. Fourteen incredible children had breathed love into me. Larry was right. It was possible. Not as I had imagined it, but nonetheless, in a most fabulous way. At this moment, I realized that if hurt people hurt people, well then, it was also true that loving people could make more love in the world. Thank God.

CHAPTER NINE

WHEN LOVE GRIEVES

Awakening to the full illumination of high desert sunshine, I scuttled like a crab retreating below the blankets for reprieve. It had been a rough week in my classroom, one in which a student had experienced a violent seizure during art class. While urgently attending to his safety and well-being, I missed that another student was processing this terrifying event by dumping an entire bottle of red tempura paint over her head.

My remedy for the weight of such stress was to take a day trip up to Virginia City. Receiving a comforting hug from Red Dog paired with more tales about Julia Bulette sounded like the best medicine for my frazzled teacher soul.

Still buried under the sheets, I playfully imagined Bulette chatting up a mustached fellow while sipping on a bourbon sour at the Union Brewery. She wore a slightly pulled-down brown felt fedora with three pheasant feathers tucked below a blue ribbon. I pictured her waiting for me to arrive around lunchtime for a private chat in her salon about the business of love.

Casting the blankets off onto the floor, I reached my hands toward the ceiling, a praying pilgrim. I wanted to engage so badly in this conversation with Bulette, but seemingly, I was a decade or two too late. Or was I? What harm would be done in writing the madame a letter and leaving it on her gravestone?

With steaming coffee in hand, I scribed a letter, a love letter, to Julia Bulette:

Madame Bulette,

I'm writing to you, Miss Julia, with hopeful reticence regarding the fate of love in the world. You see, I've never been in love and have wondered for years if it would be in my fate to find a lover practiced in the art of loving. I'm afraid the trade of love is universally dying in hearts across the globe, as people fail to remember that love is the sole purpose of our existence. We have forgotten that we are the catalysts for love's increase or decrease, instead placing ownership and blame onto circumstances outside of ourselves.

Since my first visit to your city three years ago, I've been graced with many serendipitous meetings. A cohort of unusual counselors, including fourteen children, presented themselves to me, all of whom have ushered me over the initial threshold of love. Each one of these beings has acted as a docent, delivering fundamental lessons on love to my heart's door.

Humanity holds the weight of so much pain and suffering. We sit submerged in darkness, unable to access a deep breath of truth waiting just above the waterline. Love has become a form of satire, a dubious comedy of sorts, where everyone plays Victim to the Fool. I almost fell prey to this as well, and I want to prevent others from the perils of believing that love is dead.

Miss Julia, since you were a successful and savvy entrepreneur in the business of passion, I am asking for your help and guidance as I encounter my own tribulations. More importantly, I ask for your presence to heal the heart of the world that is broken.

How do you make love in a time that is filled with misery and misfortune? You were able to unite a town ravaged by greed, poverty, addiction, and faithlessness, with your smile, your touch, and your charity. Inspired and beholden, I write to you as a woman who aims to save love. Will you please aid and abet my calling, as one woman to another, who knows the value of making more love? It's ever so needed.

Delivered in gratitude with heart,

Julia Harriet

I carefully folded the letter and placed it in an envelope. Adding a little blush to my cheeks and fine lines above my lashes, I grinned, still ruminating on my fantasy vision of meeting up with Bulette for lunch in Virginia City, where it was easy to believe that the strange and unusual were not just possible, but imminently probable.

Flying up the Geiger Grade with grace and ease, it felt as though the Goddesses were clearing a sure path for me to deliver the grandest wish my heart had ever conjured. I intentionally parked on D Street, now knowing where Julia Bulette's house was and where James and I had originally bumped into Red Dog on our first visit.

My feet were barely on the boardwalk when I heard my friend's raspy voice bellowing out some joke about the 49ers. As soon as I entered the doorway, Red Dog pivoted and let out a whoop of joy.

"Well, surprise, surprise! If it ain't my sweet Julia coming to give me a Sunday blessing. Oh, wait, it's only goddamn Saturday. Ha!"

Red Dog was in fine form, sipping from a freshly made Greyhound for brunch.

"I'm up here on a mission today, friend, and hope you can help," I said, putting my butt on the barstool next to him. "I've written a letter to Julia Bulette and want to leave it on her grave. Can you take me there?"

Red Dog rubbed his fuzzy cheeks in contemplation. It was as though he traversed a map behind closed eyes, his head darting back and forth, scrolling through memories for the exact location.

"Yep, know right where she be laid to rest. Let's suck down these drinks and head down before I be forgettin'."

We put our coats on and walked down the street toward the Silver Terrace Cemetery. The allure of a haunted grave-yard is hard to deny, and Virginia City has one of the nation's best. The town's tumultuous history was engraved upon the tombstones of its prior inhabitants. No one was spared from the wrath of rampant disease, high-stakes dereliction, and dangerous weather conditions, not to mention the battering that comes from working in a mine or just trying to survive the times. Victorian-style white fencing and monumental marble headstones demonstrated that wealth could some-times be gained by taking a gamble.

We hadn't spoken since leaving the bar, but once we entered the cemetery, I broke the silence.

"Red Dog, will you tell me a bit more about Bulette? I'm curious to know how and why she died."

"I can tell you this. She was killed by a coward who followed her home one January night. She'd gone to see a play at the opera house 'cause her lover was the big star of the show that came all the way from San Francisco. Bulette got tossed out the door 'cause someone didn't like that she was a Red Light Lady. This pissed her off real good, as she'd been promised a box seat. Storming home, she caught the attention of a greedy little French guy, Millain, and he snuck in her place after she'd gone to bed and killed her in cold blood."

A chill slid down my spine. I felt as if I'd been stabbed. My chest started pounding. Scrambling to regain composure, I looked down at the engraving on a headstone.

Evelyn Jane Hatfield
Born Dec. 24 1878
Died Dec. 25 1878
An angel visited earth and took a flower away

I suddenly and unexpectedly dropped to my knees.

"Julia, Miss Julia, you OK?" Red Dog shouted. "What the hell just happened?!"

"No." I shook my head. "No, I'm not OK, Red Dog. I did something terrible a few years ago. The choice I made has come back to haunt me in this graveyard, and I feel like the darkness of it might consume me."

"Jesus Christ, girl, what are you talking about? What's happenin' with you? You gotta give me somethin' to work with 'cause you're scaring the shit outta me."

I had no idea how to explain myself because I had sworn to never speak about the evil I had committed. I felt ripped apart, torn inside out. I could see I was giving Red Dog a real fright, so I asked him in a fragile voice, "Red Dog, have you ever done something so terrible that it made you want to die yourself?"

He lowered himself to the ground slowly so that we could be eye to eye. Grabbing my face into his leathery hands, his totally lucid voice inches from my nose, he said,

"Julia, yes, I have. I was a door gunner on a Huey Helicopter in 'Nam. I witnessed and caused more death from 1969 to 1970 than any man should know. I killed mamas holding screaming babies. I put herds of men in their graves every damn day. That was my job. To try and get us through a fucking day without ending up dead like Charlie too."

I wrapped my arms so tightly around his torso, it felt as though I would break him. Both deep into our pain, we knew we were holding each other for dear life.

The sound of our collective weeping was worthy of waking the sleeping spirits that surrounded us. We wiped each other's tears—two soldiers from different wars—until there were no more tears left to spill.

"I don't know what I'd do without you at this moment, Red Dog. I think I'm going to be OK. Hard to know, though, 'cause I'm scared shitless to own what I've done."

"I dunno, Julia. I just dunno about much at all these days, but I do know you gotta face your demons. You can't run or hide from what you've done. You gotta sit with it like you woulda hurtin' friend. Just like us fools here, plopped down in this ole burial ground. You gotta grieve what you've lost. Grieve what you've done. Otherwise, it haunts you like an angry ghost around every corner."

We lifted each other off the ground and embraced, two lost souls that were a step closer to being found.

"What should we do about the letter? Are we close to Julia's grave?"

"Yes, ma'am. I can see it from here. Let's complete this mission and go have a fucking drink. Look what you've done to me. Made an old man cry like this. You're buyin'."

I followed Red Dog to Bulette's grave. It was just as I had pictured it. Someone had left fresh red roses, and there were trinkets and costume jewelry decorating the site.

"Here you go, Madame Bulette. A love letter from me, Julia Harriet." I placed my letter against an arrangement of flowers. "May your soul find peace, and may we bring love back into the hearts of mankind."

"Amen." Red Dog wiped the remnant of a tear off his cheek. "Now, let's get the hell outta here before we end up laying in our own damn graves."

CHAPTER TEN

WHEN LOVE WRITES BACK

Black is said to be the sum of all colors when combining a mixture of pigments, and if you looked into my closet, it was definitely predominant across all avenues of my wardrobe. This boded well for the theme of the night's gathering, the Little Black Dress Cocktail Party. It was a fellow teacher's birthday, and she had gone all out by inviting the entire staff of the school and their mates to a festive and rather formal occasion at her house.

Teachers are generally not known for their dress-up skills or their ability to make small talk unless it is to gripe about students and their parents. My recent exploits up to Virginia City gave me a significant edge at being a high point in the evening's entertainment. As innocuous as teaching is, it seems all teachers need to imbibe in a little smut talk outside of school.

"Hilary, Megan, how the heck are you both? Nice to see you somewhere other than in the kids' lunchroom."

"Julia, yes, it certainly is a treat to shed our draconian teacher personas for a night out."

"Anything that gets us out of those cheap-ass yoga pants is certainly a win these days."

The two ladies nodded in agreement and smiled like Cheshire cats, flashing Merlot-stained lips and teeth.

I jumped right in, opening with a question. "Could I share a real Wild West doozy of a story that happened to me just east of town?"

Given they were both native Nevadans, my offer piqued their curiosity, apparent in their crisp raised brows.

"We'd love to hear something beyond economic unrest and mindless sports stats, so give it to us, Julia."

Teacher people are stereotypically cynical, as though they've already digested every story in existence. I knew I had to just jump in the deep end and test the waters with them.

"First off, what do you think about the concept of having past lives?"

Hilary and Megan both took a sip of wine, and like two queens on a playing card, one looked up and the other looked down.

Megan spoke up first. "Well, I guess so. I mean, I totally believe in ghosts. Is that kinda the same thing?"

"I don't know, Julia," Hilary interjected with an authoritative voice. "Like, if I'm being honest, I'm pretty sure we just croak and turn to dirt. The whole concept of reincarna-tion sounds like mumbo jumbo to me."

"I totally get it, Hilary. And Megan, I'm not sure it's the same as ghosts, but let me share a story. This young woman walked into a small town where she'd never been before and a man, a drunk man, came right up to her and insisted that he knew her already. And then he addressed her by name before she'd been introduced!"

I was really hoping for total buy-in at this point.

"Well, that's just fucking weird, Julia. Is this about you? Weren't you creeped out?!" Hilary clenched her jaw tightly as though she felt the pain herself.

This was my first real test to see how strongly I believed my own story that kept unfolding after my first visit to Virginia City. I had liquid courage, which didn't hurt, but to fully claim in front of colleagues that I was a time-traveling freak, a phantom hooker of sorts, was an entirely new expe-rience for me.

"Sure, I was suspicious at first. My boyfriend and I had just parked in Virginia City for a day's adventure. Having a stranger's sudden interest was easy to write off as a ploy for spare change. But when he called me Julia, as though he did in fact know me, a light switched on. It triggered something beyond his streetside explanation of my past life connection with a former madame, Julia Bulette. A voice deep inside of me concurred and told me to remain curious and listen."

"So, if you were really Virginia City's 'Red-Light Lady' of the 1860s, then how the hell would anyone be able to tell that by looking at you now? You don't exactly give the streetwalker vibe, so it makes me wonder how that random guy knew you were Julia Bulette."

Hilary's question made me pause. I didn't have a logical answer, and I figured it would be hard for her to accept the legitimacy of what I was saying without hard evidence or a clear explanation.

"I don't know. For me, the mystery adds validity to what I'm saying because there isn't an apparent conclusion. All I can tell you is that my life has entirely shifted because of this man declaring that I was Bulette. I keep meeting people who have some relation to Virginia City, all of whom end up teaching me a valuable lesson about love. Something's going on, and though I'm unclear why, I know it's making me a better person."

We stood all together in silence until Megan attempted to lighten up the conversation.

"Well, I've watched that ghost show set up in Virginia City, and it looks legit to me. I say if people want to think you're the reincarnation of the town's whore, then why fight 'em? Sounds more exciting than what most of us have going here."

Hilary slipped off into another conversation about the upcoming fifth-grade graduation ceremony, and Megan went back to the kitchen to refill her drink.

Now standing alone, it registered that my story clearly wasn't for everyone. Heck, I wasn't even sure where it was taking me. But given my most recent revelation with Red

Dog in the cemetery, I wasn't looking for affirmation from the outside world. With the guidance of a few close friends, I was starting to have a real sense of what love was and what it wasn't. That was good enough for me.

Returning home, I slipped out of my cocktail dress and into my cozy pajamas. Pouring a final glass of wine to enjoy on the sofa, I opened my journal to finish the day with a few reflections. But something arrested my pen and told me to close my eyes. When I did, I saw Julia Bulette sitting at a colonial-style wooden desk, scribing me a letter in return for the one I had left upon her gravesite.

Dearest Julia Harriet,

When you choose to live with your heart beating outside of your armor, you'll be like a spawning salmon, churning against stones that once protected your existence.

You will fight against the penetrating current, and it will hurt. Stripped of the pretty muscle that helped you out to sea, your atrophy will scare you. Peering into the mirror of your impending doom, you must keep swimming. Through ebbs and flows, until you reach the calm pool where you release and return life to the waiting sand.

Down to mere bones, your journey wasn't in vain, for you made it back to the place where you were born, to tuck the next generation into bed for safekeeping.

That's why you started upstream to begin with.
To complete the legacy of love that you are here to live.
To return home, again and again.

Faithfully yours,

Mme Bulette

My eyes shot open. I had seen an actual letter in my mind, her response to me, and though it wasn't on paper, I had clearly received it. Moving quickly in an attempt to write what I could remember, I spilled a splash of wine in my journal, coloring the page perfectly for the input of fresh love language. I captured what I could, reading it over several times to try and fill in gaps and missing words.

Shutting my journal carefully, as if it were one of the first biblical texts in construction, I decided to place it next to me in bed. I could feel something was about to give way, and I needed to be close enough to catch it.

CHAPTER ELEVEN

WHEN LOVE EXONERATES

"Friend, grab your bag. It's time to hop aboard!"

I couldn't have been more ecstatic to introduce my best friend Heather to the romance of train travel with our final destination being Virginia City. I'd flown to Portland, Oregon, so the two of us could take the train together to my place in Reno then on to Virginia City. I envisioned us sharing heartfelt laughs with amiable strangers on the train while cruising southbound to Reno for a weekend to remember.

Once settled into our seats, we opened a bottle of wine that I had nestled down into my clothes in anticipation of our overnight adventure. Next to the bottle, I had placed my journal and a pen, hoping to receive more divination from Julia Bulette along the way.

As I poured from the bottle of Malbec, I glanced across the aisle, catching the face of trouble in the corner of my eye. There, crouched awkwardly behind a seat, was a woman in her late thirties with open sores speckling her sullen cheeks and unkempt hair that fell on her face. This was exactly the type of character I would go out of my way to avoid on the street, and here I was within an arm's reach of crazy.

Regrettably, she spoke. "Hey, don't be a stingy bitch over there. Pour me some of that wine you got. Or else I'll come and help myself."

My stomach knotted; my hopes hit the carpeted floor of the passenger car. As a semi-seasoned traveler, I had seen enough to know this lady could quickly become a major problem for us. But I didn't want Heather to know just how much of a threat I deemed this woman to be, so I tried to de-escalate the situation.

"Sure, I'd love to pour you a glass. Do you have a cup?"

The woman wrestled through the contents of a mangled-looking grocery bag and grabbed an empty water bottle. Throwing it at me, the bottle bounced off my knee, rico-cheting from the window into Heather's lap. It was clear we were fucked.

With surgeon-like precision, I trickled wine into the plastic bottle. Once two-thirds filled, I handed it carefully back to her wearing a petrified smile.

"Don't worry, I see where you bitches hide your booze, so I'll be back to help myself. Cunts."

She got up, sucked down a gulp of wine, and wandered toward the lounge car, banging back and forth between the seats along the way.

"Fuck," Heather acknowledged, "we could be in real danger here, Julia. I think that lady is messed up on some hard-core drugs, and now she has us on her radar."

"I swear, nothing like this has happened to me before on the train. But don't worry. I won't let this whacked-out woman screw up our special time together. I'll figure out something."

Honestly, I had no idea what to do. I actually feared she might hurt us for no reason other than that we were in the wrong place at the right time. Shutting my eyes, I asked for help and protection. Suddenly, the conductor appeared in the car. He was about our age, with stout shoulders and warm brown eyes. Given the woman was still gone from our passenger car, now was the time to act.

"Excuse me, sir. My friend and I are having a problem with a woman who was sitting in the seat across the aisle from us. She verbally threatened us, and she's generally just making us feel unsafe with her language and behavior."

The conductor placed his large hand on his smooth chin, sizing up his next move while also studying me and Heather to see what we were all about. I could tell he was interested in Heather, and honestly, I hoped this might help us get a resolution regarding this woman.

"OK, so what does she—"

An argument interrupted his inquiry. The crazy woman was standing in the doorway to our train car yelling at a man and woman attempting to pass through. The conductor rushed toward the situation, pulling the woman off the man, now visibly shaken from this altercation.

I was overcome with distress upon witnessing this and started crying. There was nowhere to run or even hide from this woman's wrath. As much as I wanted to believe love could shine from everyone's hearts, the void in this woman's was so deep that no light could be seen. Five feet away, grinding her teeth as she mumbled threats to me, I felt her desire to physically assault me, to place all of her torment outside of herself onto someone else. I was the closest target. I begged myself to stop crying, knowing this instinctual fear response was inciting her further.

Closing my eyes again, to create what space I could between her suffering and my tenderness, I called out to Bulette. Imagining some of the situations she managed in her salon with violent, drunken men, I knew she was the person to consult in this moment of reckoning. Grabbing my journal from the bag between my knees, I desperately scribbled out a note like a hostage penning her last words.

Madame Bulette,

> *Sorry to be a bother, but I am pleading for your help in a moment of panic. I find myself in the proximity of a woman so overcome with misery that she has decided to threaten not only my hopes for a joyful day*

but my very existence. She appears to be loveless, and I fear perhaps even soulless at this point. How does love deal with hate? Please guide me toward the best solution for all in this situation.

With appreciation,

Julia Harriet

Heather grabbed my arm firmly and pointed discretely out the window. I hadn't noticed the train had been slowing down as it approached a station. I put my journal back into my bag and observed as we rolled in. Two police cars were sitting next to the tracks. I had to believe they were waiting to take the woman.

The conductor reappeared, but this time with an officer behind him.

"Ma'am, you'll be coming with me."

The policeman grabbed the woman's disheveled bag, much to her misgiving, and escorted her assertively down the steps as she continued to struggle and curse. Heather and I pressed up against the window to watch the drama unfold. One officer took the woman by the arm, placing her into his vehicle, while the other searched her bag on the car hood, revealing a collection of small plastic baggies filled with an unidentifiable substance. Heather and I fell into each other's arms as the train jolted forward.

Several people in our train car cheered as we regained speed down the tracks. The conductor reappeared, wearing a proud-looking grin directed at us.

"Looks like you two ladies helped bust a drug dealer. That's going to get you an immediate upgrade to a couple of first-class seats."

Heather and I collapsed back into each other's arms as a wave of relief washed over us. Grabbing our bags and happily marching up to the exclusive lounge car, I reveled in the victorious feeling of this moment, feeling like we were true champions of the Wild West.

"What do you think will happen to her?" Heather asked while peering into the darkness looming beyond the reflective glass.

The conductor paused. I did too. There was no way of really knowing.

"Not sure," I said. "There's always a painful history that brings someone to behave like that. We can only hope that she finds help to get back on track with love. But damn, I'm glad you kicked her ass off this train today because she was definitely killing our fun."

We toasted to the layers of truth held in friendship. And we kept on drinking as the train shuddered down the tracks somewhere in the vastness of Northern California headed to Sacramento. The sound of my alarm buzzing startled me out of my second hour of sleep. We were approaching our 4:30 a.m. stop to switch to the train that would take us to Reno.

"Heather, wake up, friend. We gotta get off the train soon. We're almost to Sacramento."

I heard Heather whisper to someone and realized she was with the conductor in the bunk below me. Flipping on an overhead light, we all started giggling, disoriented, still under the influence of copious wine consumption. Throwing our stuff wildly back into our bags, Heather kissed the conductor, and we stumbled off the train. Watching it roll on, we went in search of a latte to help recuperate for our next leg of the adventure across the Sierras.

"How about we sleep off yesterday on the ride to Reno so we're ready to rally when we get up to Virginia City?" Heather said, slumping in exhaustion.

I looked like I had seen brighter pastures myself. "Yes, that's exactly what I want too. Let's definitely hit the reset button."

We had crafted a solid recovery plan and were ready to execute it. As we waited on the platform in our fragile condition, a gateman approached to check our tickets. He wore a sly little smirk that immediately caught my attention as though he knew something we didn't know.

"You ladies headed to Reno, correct?"

"Yep, we're really looking forward to a peaceful trip across the mountains."

Like a quartz crystal catching the sun, he shot me a jovial little wink and pointed to a spot on the platform.

"You two, right here for Reno. You're in for a real treat. Have fun, ladies, and don't do anything I wouldn't do."

The train rumbled in with bells dinging and people bustling toward opening doors. Heather and I were the only two people being ushered into an entire train car. Upon entering, we were engulfed by the scent of roasted jalapenos and melted jack cheese. Explosive laughter echoed around a corner from which three enthusiastic women emerged. They were adorned in colorful head wraps that accentuated the richness of their espresso-colored faces.

"Oh, look at you two little sweet peas," one of them said when they saw us. "My name is Anita, and I'm happy to welcome you to the Roberts family reunion! There are so many of us packed in here that you're gonna spend this whole trip just meetin' everybody. We are all one big, happy family from the Bay, and we rented this whole damn train car to party our asses off on our way to Reno. Now, let's hurry up and grab you some ice-cold drinks."

We took the drinks like two wide-eyed eighteen-year-olds at a college party then went upstairs to meet our newly designated train family. All total, there were about fifty people: brothers, uncles, cousins, two grandmas, and a lot of aunties. Whether or not we were ready, Heather and I knew we had just stepped into a gold mine of pure love. Hugs flowed as readily as the sangria, and each person welcomed us with enthusiasm and a unique introduction.

As we made our way toward Lake Tahoe, Heather and I headed to the observation car for a better view. The lounge was filled with people reading books, sipping beverages, and enjoying the gorgeous scenery. We bumped into a table of our new friends who were playing a game of poker near the staircase down to the café then heard shouting from below.

"Oh, fuck you, motherfucker!! I'm going to kill you!!" hollered someone from the stairwell. Then we heard, "Not if I kill you first!" followed by the brutal sound of fists against flesh and bodies slamming against walls. The previously contented passengers erupted into total mayhem. One of our new friends leaped up from the card table to intervene, bravely throwing himself between flying punches and kicking legs to try and halt the madness.

"Save us, Lord! The Negroes have started a riot on the train," shrieked an elderly white woman as she scuttled by in horror. The large crowd had totally scattered to the adjoining cars. Heather and I were stunned by how fast it all happened then felt the train screech to a stop in the middle of nowhere west of Tahoe.

Our courageous friend stood between two angry-looking white men, all of them splattered in blood. Three conductors and a steward rushed into the car, all eyes landing on our new friend. As the only remaining witnesses in the car, Heather and I paid close attention to every word and action taken by the Amtrak employees.

"You, get down on the ground, now! Hands behind your back!" the senior conductor bellowed. Our friend did so without resistance. The two perpetrators still remained standing at the top of the stairs, wiping blood from the corners of their mouths while they kept covertly arguing.

"You've got it all wrong," I said. "That man on the ground had nothing to do with the fight other than trying to stop it. It's those two fools standing there with mangled faces that caused all of this. My friend and I witnessed the whole thing, and we're happy to tell you exactly what we saw and heard. Verbatim."

Heather and I looked around uncertainly then focused on two burly police officers coming up out of the stairwell. They walked past the two white men and straight over to our friend, who was still facedown on the ground.

"The man on the ground is innocent," Heather barked. "The fight was between these two white guys standing here. They are responsible for this whole thing. We saw it all take place and will give our word, under oath if needed, as to what really happened."

The officers ignored and immediately conferred with the conductors as Heather and I stared at each other in consternation.

Heather confessed in my ear, "I'm really fucking scared about what's going to happen. But we can't let these assholes get away with this."

"Absolutely," I agreed.

We stood, frozen in an unknown outcome for several minutes. Then, without words, the police abruptly grabbed the two battered white men and hauled them down the steps of the train. Once the police were out of sight, our friend slowly got up off the ground wearing a huge smile. The three of us huddled together, overcome with gratitude and relief, knowing that things could have gone very differently. The conductors dispersed, with one remaining to tape off the stairwell until it could be properly cleaned.

The train slowly started moving again, back on its way over the mountain. We returned to the party car, which was still overflowing with ingredients that made things right with the world. Welcomed back into the arms of this beautiful family, somewhere in the Sierra Nevada mountains, our lesson was that kinship extended much further than our hearts had ever known.

Heather and I went to our separate compartments, finally able to shift into restless sleep. I dreamed of another letter, penned by Bulette.

Dearest Julia Harriet,

Hate cannot exist where love is recognized. Remember those words when facing the dark shadows that lurk in the hearts of men. Anything and everything acting out against love is only an illusion of the mind. Never worry. You are learning to see without eyes, which will allow you to love freely without fear.

Yours truly,

Mme Bulette

CHAPTER TWELVE

WHEN LOVE WONDERS

Rebooting from the train trip was a must. There was no way in hell Heather and I were heading up to Virginia City as planned upon arriving to the Amtrak station in Reno. We had already spent most of our emotional currency on the way down from Portland, and if there was anything I fully ascertained about this old mining town, it was to expect the unexpected.

We happily crashed out at my house, nurturing ourselves with ample water, fresh food, and the comfort of a shower and clean sheets. Crawling into bed after saying good night to Heather, I allowed my mind to drift and wander. I pulled up imagery like a slot machine, showing the faces of those we had just encountered over the past 24 hours: the crazy drug lady, the conductor, Anita and her beautiful family, the mountain police officers.

Slipping from these visual snapshots into a dream state, I suddenly found myself walking into a saloon donning a Victorian-style corset and skirt. Inside this smoky lair was a cast of raucous libertines. Based on appearances, it was the mid-1800s, but Red Dog was there perched at his usual spot at the bar. He gestured for me to join him, and I sat carefully down on a tall wooden stool.

"Miss Julia, there's some bad blood flowin' over there. I think it'd be smart of us to mosey on before Big Jake flips his lid."

Over at the Faro table, where gamblers placed their wages, a group of men were undeniably agitated, especially one brute of a man sporting red hot cheeks and a sharp tongue. With a foreboding thud, he placed a large mound of chips down on the corner of the table. The other men gathered around who I assumed to be Big Jake, and a hand of cards were played out. Red Dog tugged hard on the sleeve of my velvet waistcoat. "Alright, Red, let's split. Looks like lady luck has left the building tonight."

As we approached the heavy wooden doors leading back out to the boardwalk, a skirmish broke out behind us among the men at the large table. Red Dog lifted me swiftly out of the doorway as bottles began to fly across the bar, with bodies not far behind. Looking back over my right shoulder, I saw the muzzle flash discharge from a short-barreled revolver pointed at Jake's chest followed with a violent BANG!

My eyes shot open and there I was, lying atop my sweaty sheets. My heart pulsed, and I felt nearly sick to my stomach. As much as I romanticized the Wild West and Virginia City in particular, I knew the town had seen a profusion of common brutality and murderous revenge. No one was safe from the prevailing lawlessness, not even Julia Bulette.

Jolted wide awake by my dream, I couldn't return to slumber without having more clarity about the night of Bulette's demise. Red Dog had given me a basic timeline from the night she fell prey to the sinister hands of John Millain, that French bastard who snuck into her salon. But something told me to dig deeper, even though I desperately needed rest.

I propped up my pillows and returned to my research, searching online for theories and details of the crime. Reading through pages and pages of recounts and reconstructions of the events that led up to Bulette's murder, one thing was clear, Millain may have been the fall guy for a greater plot against the madame. Because of her fame in town and modest fortune, she was a likely target, not to mention the commonplace of unfamiliar men arriving at her door without causing so much as a second look from townsfolk passing by.

Laying my phone down beside me, I came face to face with the bitter reality of Bulette's profession that I had venerated to quantify the findings of my own search for love outside of myself. I realized that all love won, bought, sought after, or conquered from another being rendered itself a potent vice in the quest to experience true connection and intimacy.

While there was no denying the inherent power in Bulette's experience of making love a lucrative business endeavor, the risk could not be laundered by a simple contractual agreement, even those in most traditional marriages. There was no safety or real security inherent between two people bound merely by wealth, prestige, or sexual arousal.

But then what did it mean to be in love? I was more confused than ever. Holding onto Bulette as my vixen mascot in the quest for love had allowed me to put the puzzle pieces together so far. Arriving at this emotional precipice, I had two choices: to leap or to lie down.

Dearest Julia Harriet,

Many maps exist for you to pull from as you plot your path across love's wild lushness. Rumi is one of my favorite guides:

"The minute I heard my first love story, I started looking for you, not knowing how blind that was. Lovers don't finally meet somewhere. They're in each other all along."

You are on the right road. Now keep going.

With admiration,

Mme Bulette

I must have fallen asleep because I was startled by the sound of Heather grinding coffee beans in my kitchen. We sipped and conversed about our day's adventure up to Virginia City. Despite my desire to show Heather around, I couldn't help but hold the profundity of my night's contemplations.

"Julia, what's weighing on you? I can tell something's up with you this morning."

Looking up from the blackness swirling in my cup, tears welled in my eyes.

"What's happening in that heart of yours, friend?"

Heather reached over and put her hand gently on my tense shoulder.

"It's…it's that, I'm in my freaking mid-twenties and I've never been in love. Not even close. And I've been trying to figure it out, Heather. But I'm terrified that there's something wrong with me."

Much like when Red Dog sat on the dusty ground of the cemetery with me, Heather swooped in, placing her chair up next to mine.

"Julia, listen to me, OK? There are a lot of people who say they are in love and claim to understand what love is. But my guess is that only about five percent of people have a clue. You're just one of the rare, honest ones out there who are brave enough to say they don't know what the hell they are doing. Here's my guess—because you are asking the question, that means you are on track to finding an answer."

Heather's words felt extremely reassuring. I envisioned most great explorers, inventors, and artists grappling with their own insecurities and quandaries as they forged the frontiers of their fields. If I considered myself one of them and switched my focus from being a hunter to a seeker of love, something would shift. It all reminded me of what Larry the silversmith spoke of over chicken dinner.

"I really appreciate your words, friend. You're right. I'm going to switch up my game and try a new approach to this loving shit. I'm going to quit chasing after love and allow it to discover me. Like in one of those National Geographic shows where the photographer gets the best shot of the lion by waiting for it to walk right up to him."

Feeling emotionally buoyed, it was time to rally up to Virginia City and show my friend what life was like in a curious little old mining town.

"I can't wait for you to meet Red Dog, Heather. He pretty much carries the pulse of the town and has a heart more genuine than anything I've ever known."

"When we find him, let's ask him about love. Do you think he's ever been in love, Julia?"

I realized I'd never seen him with a woman nor heard him speak of one from his past. How odd given the nature of our closeness over the past few years.

"I don't know. And it shocks me that I haven't a clue. Let's feel him out, for sure."

CHAPTER THIRTEEN

WHEN LOVE ARRIVES

Super Bowl Sunday. A day when the majority of Americans press pause on reality to fully invest in the outcome of a national sporting event or, if nothing else, to catch the spectacle of the half-time show. Virginia City was no different, filled with diehard fans clad in colorful jerseys, hats, and face paint. Heather and I didn't look suited to play ball with this testosterone-fueled revelry, but we were about finding Red Dog, not here hunting for a tailgate party.

Unlike love, Red Dog was quite easy to capture. He was standing up behind his signature bar stool at the Union Brewery after a bad ref call had riled him to the point of stomping and yelling. We entered the bar thundering with boos and cheers in equal measure and surprised Red Dog.

"Jesus Christ, you scared the hell out of me. I didn't even see you comin', Miss Julia."

He gave me a quicker-than-usual squeeze so he could get his eyes back on the screen.

"Hey, Red Dog, I want you to meet my friend Heather. She's visiting all the way from Portland, Oregon."

Normally Red Dog was very attentive until he was on his fifth or sixth drink. But it was the third quarter, and the game was all tied up.

"Heather, me lady. Any friend of Miss Julia is dear to me as well. Pleasure to… Oh, goddammit, that son of a bitch!"

The crowd of patrons started yelling for and against the call. Realizing there was no use in trying to reengage Red Dog, Heather and I grabbed drinks and spotted a small open table toward the back of the bar.

"We'll catch up with you in a bit when you step outside for a smoke, Red."

I'm not sure he even heard me. But this was no worry because Heather and I were quite good at entertaining ourselves.

Sipping from my glass of wine, I felt the warmth of someone's attention to my left. Turning instinctively with a "caught you" kind of whimsy on my face, I spotted a man just two tables away grinning right back. I giggled aloud and bashfully looked away, trying to regain composure and figure out what to do next. Before I had time to make a plan, he was standing right next to me.

"You look so familiar to me, and I'm trying to place where we've met before. I'm RJ. I live just down the hill in Sparks. Remind me of your name?"

Though RJ didn't look familiar in the face, I felt it in the way he spoke to me.

"I'm Julia. I'm up here from Reno, so maybe we've met around town. Seriously, your smile really reminds me of—"

The collective burst with a hearty round of whoops and cheers as a touchdown was scored to break the tie.

"Want to step outside so we can continue our conversation?"

"I'd love to." I was totally captivated by RJ and eager to unpack and understand our connection.

Scanning the room for Heather, I spotted her at the bar ordering another drink with her arm around some good-looking guy. It was perfect. We both had made a match and were equally amused.

RJ reached out to grab my hand as I rose from the chair, and I jumped at the offer, appreciative of his lead as we weaved through the dense crowd to the door. His thick palm pressing against my hand conjured a sensuality that pulled my thoughts down into my nether regions, but I resurfaced and reset my intentions, aware that the energy here had far more potential.

Exiting the bar, the cold rays of the sun caught us, a focused stage light directed at two stars of an impromptu show. RJ spun me around like we were Gene Kelly and Rita Hayworth.

Without further ado, another actor stumbled onto the stage, with his long red hair mirroring the sun's fading fire. Red Dog stole the show, barging comedically between RJ and me, spilling part of his Greyhound on RJ's pants.

"Well, no one ever said you were full of grace, Red Dog. While you're at it, meet my new friend RJ. And go grab him a napkin for your trouble."

Pulling a wad of sour-looking paper towels from his pocket, Red Dog handed them to RJ wearing a little smirk. RJ took the wad and headed back inside the bar to undoubtedly clean up with more appropriate toiletries in the bathroom.

"So, what were you kids up to out here missin' the end of the damn game?"

He was right, we were missing the biggest game of the year, but neither of us seemed to give a shit about football. RJ and I had bumped into each other. Maybe again, or maybe it was for the first time. Either way, RJ elicited a feeling in my heart that I couldn't put a name to but knew it felt thrilling. And I was pleased that it appeared that I, too, had summoned some kind of excitement in him.

"Hey there, Red Dog. Guess what? I actually just met someone who makes me feel something. Something new. May I ask how come you never seem to catch any ladies around town? You're a fun-loving guy."

By the look on his face, I had thrown a net over Red Dog that he wanted to cast off. "Now, Miss Julia, I want you to take that back. You know I ain't the courtin' type of guy.

What woman in her flippin' right mind is gonna be scootin' up next to me?"

"But you want affection and to be loved, don't you, Red?"

"I got all I be needin,' Miss Julia. A guy like me ain't deservin' because I also ain't givin'. And that's how this love shit be. You reap what you—"

"Sow," RJ interjected, reentering with a fresh drink for both of us in hand. Red Dog held a pang of jealousy in the tight corners of his mouth. Or from the strain of truth he'd just shared about giving and receiving love.

"All right, now, RJ. You look like a nice enough fella. But I thinkin' you ain't gotta clue as to who you're dealin' with here in this woman. Miss Julia ain't just an anybody FOR everybody."

Red Dog threw his whole arm sarcastically toward me, and I instantly regretted having asked him about his love life. I had pushed a rock and exposed a snake's den hidden under Red Dog's long beard.

But RJ didn't back down. In fact, he surprised me by rising to the challenge.

"I knew the moment I saw Julia that she was somebody. And not just someone special. She is a woman I've met before. Somehow, I let her slip away from me in the past, but I'm going to do my best to not let that happen again."

Frozen, as if under a spell, I stood there with my mouth slightly open.

Red Dog appeared stuck too. Sort of like he'd lost a game of poker on a hasty bluff and now had nowhere to hide his humiliation. Worse yet, the look on his face was that of a man who had played a nasty trick on himself because he couldn't run from the paradox that he had unearthed: The only way to be worthy of love was to get in the game.

"Fine enough then. I'll be lettin' you two love birds get back to peckin'. Miss Julia, be sure to give old Red a hug before you and Heather be splittin'. RJ, pleasure's mine. But don't you forget what I be tellin' you. She ain't just for anybody." And with that, Red Dog ambled back into the bar without a second look.

"I think he likes you," RJ said. "Smart man. I've got to head back down the hill soon, but as I said, I don't want to lose you again."

"I don't want you to lose me either. Here's my card. Let's keep talking."

He pulled me into a goodbye embrace, and I hung there in his arms like a woman who had discovered something she definitely wasn't willing to part with.

It wasn't long after our encounter that I received a very welcome message from this man I could and would not forget.

Hey lovely, it's RJ here – I simply can't get your face out of my mind. I've come to realize that I'd been dreaming about you for years before we grasped hands in the Union Brewery last Sunday. The familiarity of you is astounding to me. And this thing we've started here, where we speak to listen, make each other laugh, and bring out the light in each other, is very important to me.

I'll never be the same knowing you exist, and finally feeling my own existence through this knowledge. That is what you can do to a soul, Julia. Make it live for the first time. And I hope I can do the same for you, in my own way.

I like who you are as a human being, too. The world around us is ugly, but people like us hopefully make it more bearable, maybe even a happier place overall. We do this by showing up and looking deeply into each other, without need or judgment, like two kids sharing a kaleidoscope.

Let's meet for coffee soon. Text me back when you're ready.

CHAPTER FOURTEEN

WHEN LOVE TEACHES

I was almost ready for RJ, but there was one thing I had to know before I held his hand again. After years of mining through biographies of Julia Bulette, the revered Madame of Virginia City, the inner journalist in me beckoned to know firsthand how the business of love worked in a brothel. I wanted the perspective of the women who offered their services.

Maybe it was simply to quell my decades-old fascination with life as a call girl, sparked anew by watching yet another Julia brilliantly portray the role on screen in *Pretty Woman*. I refused to see my curiosity as anything other than charm and prowess. At least, that's what I was telling myself.

Calling Heather to gain her valuable perspective seemed like a logical next step.

"Hey, friend, how's it going?"

"I'm doing great. Just got a new job bartending at a pub that opened up in North Portland. What's up with you?"

"I'm working up the guts to call RJ, the guy I met on Super Bowl Sunday. He sent me the sweetest message, and I really want to see him again. But I feel like I need to do something first."

"That's so great, friend. He seemed like a true gentleman, and I'm glad you're in touch. What do you need before you reach out to him?"

"This is going to sound crazy, but bear with me. I've spent years now learning about Julia Bulette, the madame I've told you about, whom Red Dog claims that I somehow am. Well, I want to go visit an actual brothel because it's legal just outside of Reno. And I want to know what it's actually like for women who work in the business."

Silence enveloped the conversation; it was the type of flat static that made me feel as though we'd been disconnected.

"Julia, what do you mean?" Heather finally asked. "Please tell me you aren't going to an actual whorehouse. What would you do there? Show up and interview the chicks? I don't think that would go over well, and it certainly isn't safe to go to a place like that."

I inhaled deeply, knowing rationally that Heather was correct. But I wasn't going to bow down to reason that quickly.

"I totally hear you. But I have to do this, friend, or I will always wonder, and honestly, I need to know if the women who work in the sex trades are OK. I want to understand how Julia Bulette created a professional business while also offering so much love to her community."

I could tell Heather hated the idea. I couldn't blame her.

"Look, I know you're going to do what you want to do, but I really advise against it. Looking at the choice from a feminist point of view, patronizing a place like that potentially jeopardizes what so many women have done to rise out of having to sell themselves sexually to survive."

Damn, maybe I shouldn't have sought counsel.

"Thanks for your advice, Heather. I do really appreciate and hear what you're saying."

"I know you aren't going to listen to reason, so text me before you go in. I'll be sure to call the police if you go missing."

"Love you, friend."

"Love you too, you crazy nut. Please be safe."

About a half hour later, I walked up concrete steps, my knees trembling in anticipation of what might be on the other side of the oversized double doors. Judging by the empty parking lot, I was the only visitor of the Mustang Ranch at 8 a.m. on Monday morning. It was winter break, so maybe people were busy traveling with their families on vacation. Either way, I uttered a basic prayer to survive this experience and pulled open the heavy doors. A huge, biker-looking fellow spun around behind a small metal bar to size me up. He made a face, like he licked a lemon, and continued counting his till.

It looked similar to what I had imagined, although its emptiness added an element of severity to the scene. As I ordered a vodka tonic, a woman sashayed through two French doors at the back. Wearing clear stilettos, she must have been close to six feet tall, which made her presence even more powerful as she entered the room. Seeing me as the only customer, she let out a happy hoot and raised her arms in the air like a cheerleader.

"Hello, you little Monday morning morsel. What brings a princess like you into this den of inequity?"

Nervous giggles rose from my chest like the bubbles in my tumbler.

"I guess you could say I'm here to understand what this is all about."

I sounded like an idiot, and I could feel Heather's disapproval like a rain cloud overhead.

"Well, you probably know that most people come here to fuck, but it's not quite that simple. Because nothing is truly simple."

The woman sat on the barstool next to me, connecting like a statue to a pedestal.

"I'm Jenny Marie. Let's grab a bite together and talk more about what you're looking for."

Within minutes, two plates of breakfast appeared, something scrambled with eggs. I figured most people didn't come here for the food, and it showed.

"Jenny, I won't bore you with my whole story, but I'm wondering if you would mind answering a few questions?"

"Not at all, sweetie. But tell me your name."

"I'm Julia. And I'm on a quest to figure out love."

"First off, there isn't a lot of love exchanged here. Well, at least not how most people think of it. This is a place where people come to feel better, often because love did them wrong. But here, they can get whatever they need without strings attached."

"That makes sense. But I just have to know, are you and all the women here OK? Like, are you doing this work because you want to?"

"Oh shit, honey, this place is great. We all work for ourselves as independent contractors, so we set our own rates and decide who to do or not. I used to be an interior designer in Los Angeles. But I make way more money this way and, honestly, have way more fun."

"What's the downside then? Don't you ever come up against some sleazy guys who are screwed up?"

"Sure, sometimes things get weird, but we have a lot of security in here. Nobody gets out of hand. And really, there's nothing wrong with an adult woman doing whatever the hell she wants with her body. It's no different from any profession where you use your physical skills to make money."

"That makes a lot of sense. How does this work translate to your love life? Isn't it hard to date when you work as a prostitute?"

Jenny was chewing on some burnt toast and wearing a thoughtful expression.

"Sometimes men don't like it. They don't like to share or imagine their lady with anyone else. But there are guys who actually prefer it. The one thing I've learned is that you've got to love yourself doing this work, separate from being in any relationship. Love comes easy when you start by loving yourself."

"I've been learning a lot of lessons about that lately, Jenny. It's what brought me here. To try and figure out what love is made of."

"I want to show you something Julia. Are you interested?"

I went from almost comfortable to being belted with fear.

"I'm not sure what you mean, but I'm curious, and if I'm being honest, a little scared."

She pushed both our plates toward the bartender and leaned in close to me.

"Julia, come in the back with me. I want to show you one or two things I've learned about self-love."

I didn't really have a choice, both because I wanted to know what she had to show me and because I had come to a whorehouse to learn.

"OK, I'd like to see whatever it is you want to show me."

We walked through the double doors from which she had originally appeared and entered a closed courtyard with a magnificent garden, complete with full-sized trees and a large fountain with exotic floating plants.

"Just follow me."

I did, looking into every open door and around every corner. The layout was like a Mediterranean labyrinth, leading us eventually to a small room at the end of a corridor.

"Lay on the bed. By that, I mean get comfortable, and let's talk."

Jenny removed her clothes, kept her heels on, and sat in a wingback chair near the bed.

"The key to love is knowing yourself. Do you feel like you know yourself, Julia? Like both sexually and emotionally?"

The heat of embarrassment hit me.

"I'm just starting to know myself. But as much sex and as many relationships as I've had, I've never felt love or made love. I blamed the inadequacy of my relationships. Then I thought it was because something was wrong with me. But now, I'm figuring out that it's because I need to go inside my own heart and give myself compassionate care. That's why I'm here."

"Spot on, girl. You're on the right track. Want another piece of the puzzle?"

"Please, tell me."

"I can't tell you, but I can show you. Have you ever been with a woman before?"

"No, I haven't. Is that OK?" I felt safe with Jenny, and I was very curious.

"Yes, it's totally fine. I want to show you how good it can feel sexually without it being about what a guy needs or desires. This is going to be all about you. As I said, a powerful act of self-love."

"I'm ready. Show me, Jenny."

She proceeded to remove my clothes while kissing me up and down my legs. My head tried to make sense of what was happening, to judge the activities and drag me out of being present. That felt all wrong, so instead, I listened to the voice inside my heart. I heard Bulette's voice and felt her words while submitting to whatever Jenny wanted to teach me. For the first time, I surrendered to feeling total sexual pleasure, releasing control, and giving myself completely to this woman I had just met. With my eyes closed and my heart open, I *became* the experience.

When we finished, I sat up, smiling with permeating satisfaction. No embarrassment or explanations, just feeling self-aware and somehow wiser. I now knew about love being an inside job, and though there is inherent reciprocity in lovemaking, I felt the authenticity of being able to receive and give, accepting and returning without fear of compromising or being compromised.

Able to finally say a few words, I said, "Thank you for showing me how to love myself, and for teaching me that I can both give and receive love. I am committed to learning more about this self-love thing. You certainly sparked my interest."

"Bingo, girlfriend. I knew you were a quick study. And you're cute as hell too. You're going to find a man who adores you, but most importantly, who has a full cup from which to pour you infinite love. Never forget or dishonor your worth. That's your homework."

"This has been the most amazing experience. However, I better text my best friend before she calls the cops to rescue me."

"No problem. I'll walk you out."

I quickly put myself back together, and Jenny threw on a lacy purple robe. We made our way back to the French doors, where she opened her arms to me, saying, "I don't often hug when it's time to say goodbye, but you're something special. I feel honored to have been your teacher today. You take care of that heart of yours and do the things that keep it full of love."

We hugged and I said goodbye. I walked back to my car feeling the depth of a lesson I would never forget. Then it hit me. That was it! I was feeling. I was free to feel. I sat for a moment in the driver's seat assessing myself in the rearview mirror. There I was, a young woman who started out afraid, judgmental, and biased. I'd known confusion and doubt, felt joy and pain, survived self-hate, loss, and grief, and finally acquired enough understanding and confidence to try a new hand at love.

Grabbing my phone from my purse, I felt there was no better time to call RJ. I was ready. Well, first I texted Heather. But then I took the leap I'd been so afraid of taking. Trusting myself and my instincts, I left a brief message. "Hey, RJ, it's Julia. I'd love to grab a coffee. I'd love to have you take my hand while we explore the world and fill it with love. You free today?"

EPILOGUE

Madame Bulette,

Since I placed my letter on your grave, your responses have come to me in many miraculous ways, from quotes delivered off the lips of strangers to the arrival of a man that swept my heart clean away. I can't fully express the gratitude I feel for your tender and persistent guidance.

When I began my quest to learn what it meant to make love and truly fall in love, I looked everywhere but within for the answer. I couldn't fathom falling in love as an introspective journey. In fact, I had to reframe it completely, due in part to your teachings. Instead of leaping into a deep, dark pool to satisfy another person's desire, you encouraged me to swim to the shore and simply shut my eyes.

What did I see? The essence of my own heart. That's where love lived all along, separate from the churning chaos of lust and confusion of contradictory needs. Closing my eyes, I came home to a quiet center that ceased all yearning, chasing, and forcing. When love lives peacefully within me, that is also how it finds me. I am no longer forced to run toward it or away from it. I don't need to beg it to stay or push it away. Because when something is right for me, I know it now, thanks to your wise counsel.

Perhaps that's why the world loves you so, Madame. Because you saved so many from a loveless existence, from wandering the globe starving and broken from what they mistook as love. When men came to your door, you weren't simply serving them sexual satisfaction for the purpose of pain abatement. You were healing the hunger that drove men to delirium, carefully placing love back into the voids that make us singularly human.

You saved love from certain death in the perilous desert. I have come back to you now, to take the torch and carry it forth. It is time to make more love in the world by embodying it, by giving and receiving liberating love.

When it's all over, I want to be able to say, "I offered love. I received love. I was love." Thank you for taking me back into my heart to listen. I am home. You are right. I have come home to love myself first, then share it with others.

With infinite appreciation,

Julia Harriet

ACKNOWLEDGMENTS

No one writes a love story alone. *The Woman Who Saved Love* is the culmination of precious conversations gifted to me from late nights in bars, long walks with friends, and random meetings where the sidewalk ends. Along the way, I have learned that everyone holds a unique love story in their heart. When we slow down to listen and witness each other's pain, growth, hopes, and fears, the possibility of love is able to live on.

To my children, Mirabelle and Dockton, I am eternally grateful for the endless hugs and humor you delivered to me as I sat typing away at the kitchen table. You've both taught me that anything is possible with the right amount of magic, laughter, and chocolate.

To my father, Scott, for picking my kids up from school so I could keep writing and who had a glass of wine waiting at the end of a long day editing. Your belief in my ability to persist, even when things were hard beyond measure, has helped me to believe in myself.

To the powerhouse women in my life who stood by me as I turned my wild ideas into chapters drafted: Cheryl Roberts Oliver, my wordsmith and dear heart; Aunt Judy, my fierce confidant and fellow crab sister; Joy Mann, my voice of solace and wisdom; my mom, Vicki Sue, my greatest cheerleader and kindest sounding board.

To the brilliant team at Davis Creative Publishing Partners, who offered holistic support and superior counsel every step of the way in birthing this love story into creation.

And last, but certainly not least, to old Red Dog. You've been gone for some time now, but your voice and stories live on in this wisdom shared. I'm forever grateful for the tears spilled and drinks we consumed, arm in arm, like two soldiers of the heart. You sure have become an unlikely counselor of love, Old Red. I promise to keep your legacy alive by fighting the good fight for love out there in our wild world.

May we all strive to offer each other more compassion and care in these times when love can appear elusive or altogether lost. Sometimes all it takes is one hand to walk us back into the light of love waiting.

ABOUT THE AUTHOR

Julia Harriet is a wild-hearted woman with an insatiable curiosity. She is also a #1 international best-selling author, an inspirational speaker, and a builder who has been working in construction for over seven years on Vashon Island. As the mother of two incredible children, Julia loves to play outdoors, learn with her hands, and laugh with unbridled vigor.

A Monsieur Bissette,

Mandataire des Hommes de couleur de la Martinique.

Monsieur,

La classe de couleur de la Guiane française n'est pas indifférente aux nobles efforts qui caractérisent vos démarches auprès de l'autorité législative. Zélé défenseur des droits que réclame sa position actuelle, votre continuelle sollicitude est un titre sacré à sa reconnaissance.

Victime en 1824 d'un système d'injustices et d'oppressions sans exemples dans nos fastes civils, vous vous êtes attaché à combattre ce système qui pourrait à la suite devenir également funeste à vos concitoyens, si sa base n'était pas sapée; car on ne peut pas contester l'existence des Fernand de Loynes, des Davila, des Vincent de Valverde, etc., etc., de 1824, dans toutes les colonies françaises.

En prenant la défense de cette cause sacrée, vos jours se trouvent placés dans un imminent danger.

Ah! que le sacrifice eût été beau !!!... Mais si l'orage se dissipait, en vain élevant la tête pour considérer ce que vous auriez fait, quelqu'un aurait bien dit en prophétisant avec David: *De torrente in viâ bibet, proptereà exaltabit caput.*

Pour moi en particulier, je vous rends un bien mince tribut en plaçant sous votre protection les réclamations suivantes, que j'adresse à la Chambre des Députés dans l'intérêt des hommes de couleur de la Guiane française.

Daignez, Monsieur, agréer ce faible hommage de ma reconnaissance, et c'est avec un profond respect que je suis

Votre dévoué serviteur,

F.-F. LE BLOND.

Avis préliminaire.

Que l'on ne s'attende pas à trouver dans cet écrit un style brillant, et bien moins un monument historique pour la postérité; je sais que mes faibles lumières sont une cause efficiente qui aurait dû m'empêcher d'écrire. Mais la vérité n'est-elle pas la même partout?

Abreuvé d'opprobre et d'avilissement, frappé de réprobation et accablé sous le poids des humiliations, j'ai dû prendre la plume pour en tracer le fidèle tableau. C'est aux nobles dispensateurs des lois que j'offre cet écrit, c'est à vous, de Tracy, Laborde, Salverte, Lafayette, Laisné de Villevêque, etc. Si du moins il n'éclaire pas entièrement votre religion sur les besoins généraux de la Guiane française, vous y puiserez toujours des renseignements, qui seront de quelqu'intérêts dans vos discutions législatives.

En prenant la plume, aucun esprit de parti ne m'a dirigé dans cet écrit.

Quant aux faits que j'ai tracés ils sont avérés. Je me suis abstenu d'entrer dans une description générale touchant l'administration de cette colonie et les injustices qui la caractérisent : une plume plus éloquente s'est chargée de cette mission.

Que sais-je, il est possible que ma voix soit trop tardive : la discution est peut-être ouverte dans ce moment, notre sort déjà fixé !!! C'est ce que j'ignore actuellement, mais j'aurai du moins la satisfaction d'avoir dit quelque chose.

Ne voulant parler que de certaines réclamations, je n'ai pas dû entrer dans l'énumération des faits qui caractérisent les préjugés jusqu'à Napoléon. Il me suffira de dire que, depuis plus d'un siècle, de vives demandes n'ont pas cessé de réveiller l'attention du gouvernement métropolitain : les monuments de ces réclamations subsistent encore, mais le ministère de la marine a toujours été obsédé par la faction coloniale.

> La seule indifférence
> Fut tout le partage
> De ces réclamations
> Qui vieillissent dans les cartons.

Nous avons le code noir qui suffit seul pour immortaliser le grand Colbert. Mais la population des colonies ignore jusqu'à ce jour si ce code existe ; car son application a toujours été entravée par les administrateurs qui ont successivement régi ces contrées.

OBSERVATIONS

SUR

L'ÉTAT POLITIQUE

DES

HOMMES DE COULEUR

DE LA GUIANE FRANÇAISE.

———

L'Eternel dans ses mains tient seul nos destinées,
Il sait, quand il lui plait, veiller sur nos années.
VOLTAIRE. *La Henriade.*

Napoléon ayant été proclamé empereur, la révolution de 89 qui nous avait procuré un moment de liberté fut anéantie ; dès lors, ont recommencé ces vexations de tout genre, ces barbaries inconnues chez les peuples civilisés, que M. Bissette signale avec force à l'attention des Chambres, en demandant leur anéantissement définitif.

L'homme qui avait asservi l'univers, ne réfléchit pas à l'inévitable conséquence que cette domination dut entraîner, et succomba. Il fit place à Louis XVIII, l'auteur de la Charte : la classe de couleur ne devant aucune amélioration à ce monarque, rien ne m'oblige d'en parler. Mais environ dix ans après son avénement, il mourut ; Charles X de funeste mémoire lui succéda. Aucun changement n'a eu lieu pendant ces trois règnes successifs.

La glorieuse révolution de juillet arriva. Le peuple trop long-temps opprimé ne vit son salut que dans la chûte d'un monarque incapable d'être à la tête de ses intérêts, et le fit descendre du trône où le titre de ses ancêtres l'avait appelé.

Ici, mon admiration est inexprimable, en considérant cette

belle Franee devenue aujourd'hui la Rome des Scipion , et la Grèce de Milthiade et de Léonidas !

La Charte de Louis XVIII fut amendée dans l'intérêt général du grand peuple Français. Louis-Philippe , vainqueur de Jemmapes et de Valmy , que 38 ans d'intervalle n'avaient pas effacé du souvenir de la France, fut appelé le 3o juillet, comme Lieutenant-Général du royaume.

Les dépositaires des destinées de la nation , voulant éviter les désastreuses conséquences de la révolution de 89, le proclamèrent Roi des Français , le 9 août, aux cris d'un enthousiasme général. La couronne fut acceptée par lui, et il fit entendre ces paroles sublimes : « La Charte sera désormais une vérité. »

Je ne dois m'arrêter qu'aux deux articles sur lesquels je base les réclamations suivantes, qu'exige notre état social.

« Les Français, dit l'article premier de la Charte , sont égaux devant la loi, quels que soient d'ailleurs leurs titres et leurs rangs. »

Demande. Quelles sont les possessions que nous habitons?

Réponse. Celles de la France.

D. Nous sommes donc Français?

R. Oui, puisque nous sommes nés sur ce territoire : nous y avons formé des établissements de commerce et de culture, conséquemment nous y avons acquis les droits de citoyens français.

D. L'article premier établit-il une différence entre les castes qui doivent jouir des droits civils, et celles qui doivent en être privées ?

R. Non.

D. Pourquoi la classe de couleur qui contribue aux charges publiques , qui fait fleurir l'agriculture, etc., etc., est-elle entravée dans la jouissance de ses droits ?

R. C'est l'absurde préjugé colonial qui a posé ces entraves, en se basant sur l'article 73 de l'ancienne Charte, qui dit: « Les Colonies seront régies par des lois et des réglements particuliers. »

Lequel article est faussement interprété dans les Colonies.

Ecoutons l'article 64 de la Charte de 1830 : *Les Colonies se-*
ront régies par des lois particulières.

On ne peut donc faire application aujourd'hui de ces mots ,
qui furent la base du despotisme, *et réglements particuliers.*

Cependant notre sort n'est point changé, les mêmes injustices
subsistent dans les Colonies; vainement la publication de l'ordonnance royale du 24 février 1831 a eu lieu : à Cayenne l'on pourrait contester avec raison l'existence d'un nouvel ordre politique.

Ainsi la Guiane française ne doit pas rester indifférente aux
sollicitations soumises à la décision des Chambres : la classe
de couleur s'empresse par ma voix de faire connaître sa position ,
sur laquelle on prendra une base certaine pour fixer une sage
institution. Les hommes de couleur de la Martinique, de la
Guadeloupe et de l'île Bourbon , ont fait parvenir leurs réclamations par l'organe de leurs mandataires. Cayenne laissera-
t-elle ainsi régler son sort sans en rien dire? La classe de
couleur de la Guiane n'a-t-elle aucune réclamation à faire?
Les lois coloniales n'exercent-elles pas leur funeste influence
ici comme aux Antilles? J'entends : humiliés depuis longues
années , les hommes de couleur croient que la voie des réclamations est toujours interceptée pour eux. Le pouvoir de l'aris-
tocratie coloniale , il est vrai, place pour ainsi dire à l'index
inquisitorial ceux qui osent élever la voix pour réclamer leurs
droits naturels; mais il y a cependant d'honorables exceptions
à faire dans ce pays. Il est malheureux que ceux mêmes qui
ont des dispositions conciliatrices soient souvent influencés par
cette terrible faction; c'est ainsi que le métropolitain qui arrive
dans ces contrées lointaines est de suite gagné, rarement il
évite ces piéges, les gouverneurs mêmes en sont victimes :

Ils boivent à longs traits l'oubli de leur devoir.

Au reste on ne peut avoir mauvaise grâce à réclamer des
droits que la nature a concédés à tous.

Ainsi, je vais essayer, non de dénoncer tous les abus qui
nous oppriment actuellement, l'entreprise est trop épineuse;
mais seulement de demander l'anéantissement dans la nou-

velle législation qu'on prépare aux colonies, des lois qui pèsent sur notre destinée : ensuite j'exposerai de quelle manière on peut fixer le cens électoral, en ayant égard à la médiocrité des fortunes de ce pays.

La Guiane française, quoique moins peuplée que les autres colonies, est cependant une des premières terres que reconnut Christophe Colomb, en 1498 : l'année suivante, Améric Vespuce se dirigea vers l'Orénoque. Elle comporte une étendue de côtes d'environ 70 lieues ; autrefois elle en comptait plus de 150, car ses limites à l'est étaient la rivière d'Aragouary ; mais dans une longue contestation qui a eu lieu entre les cours de France et du Brésil, cette dernière nous fit prendre la détermination d'abandonner toute la portion comprise entre l'Aragouary et l'Oyapock : ainsi donc, la Guyanne portugaise fut augmentée aux dépens de la nôtre. La profondeur de cette vaste région a toujours varié d'après ceux qui l'ont parcourue. Quelques Français tentèrent le premier établissement en 1604 ; elle fut prise et pillée par les Anglais en 1667 ; elle passa 7 ans après, c'est-à-dire en 1674, sous la protection du roi de France. Quoiqu'elle fut conquise par les Hollandais en 1678, et par les Portugais en 1809, cependant dès 1674 on peut considérer ce pays comme colonie française. Cayenne en est le chef-lieu, elle est à 54° 36' de longitude O, et à 4° 56' de latitude N ; sa population est évaluée aujourd'hui à 23,047 individus de toutes les classes, dont 3,786 de condition libre, et 19,261 esclaves.

Je ne me suis arrêté à ces petits détails que pour faire connaître à peu près sa naissance et sa faible population.

Avant la révolution de 89, la classe de couleur de la Guiane française n'était composée que d'environ 6 à 700 personnes libres ; en 1820, elle était arrivée à 1,733 ; aujourd'hui elle est composée d'environ 2,300. Dans les temps antérieurs à la glorieuse révolution de 89, elle était courbée sous le despotisme colonial, mais l'ordonnance inconstitutionnelle du 1er vendémiaire n'avait pas parue.

Cette révolution donc, apporta quelque consolation à cette

classe qui vivait dans le plus complet découragement ; elle avait reconnu dès-lors qu'elle était née pour faire partie de la grande famille européenne. Les liens légitimes furent la base de son émulation ; l'accroissement devenait prodigieux au grand déplaisir des colons.

A la voix du colosse qui pesait sur le monde, la liberté fut anéantie. M. Victor Hugues arriva dans la colonie comme administrateur : les colons blancs, effrayés naguères des progrès d'une classe qui devait à la suite balancer l'influence qu'ils exerçaient, applaudirent au choix du monarque.

M. Victor Hugues ne trompa pas leur attente. Il avait cependant tout le mérite qui caractérise un excellent administrateur, mais par malheur sa condescendance fut grande pour les habitants : entouré et pressé de toute part, il a dû céder. Soudain la classe de couleur fut proscrite ; en même temps ont pris naissance cette foule d'arrêtés, d'ordonnances et de réglements, base de toutes les injustices exercées depuis ce temps-là.

Le code civil fut publié à la Guiane française, avec des modifications qu'exigeaient, dit-on, les localités ; c'est ainsi que la métropole a toujours été le jouet d'un despotisme absolu et sans frein. On sait, et je ne crains pas de le répéter, *que les rois qu'on trompe de près, on les trompe encore mieux de loin ; qu'il est aisé d'en obtenir par le mensonge et la surprise, des ordres dont ils frémiraient, s'ils en prévoyaient les abus.*

M. Victor Hugues donc (puisque nous ne devons nommer que lui) fort de la distance de 1800 lieues, qui séparent la colonie de la mère patrie, donna un libre cours aux rigueurs d'un arbitraire violent. On impute à des collaborateurs les actes illégaux de son administration, cela est vrai ; mais si les chefs pouvaient faire tomber sur ces derniers toutes les conséquences de l'injustice, Charles X serait encore assis sur le trône de France, ses ministres seuls auraient encouru la disgrâce du peuple français : dès-lors, l'imputation reste personnelle au lieu d'être particulière.

Les hommes de couleur basant leurs réclamations sur les articles 1er et 64 de la nouvelle Charte, demandent l'abrogation de tous les arrêtés coloniaux qui les ont privés de l'exercice des droits civils et politiques jusqu'à la révolution de juillet, comme incompatibles avec le sentiment de philantropie de la France régénérée, et particulièrement de l'ordonnance du 1er vendémiaire an XIII, qui a modifié le code civil à la Guiane française, ainsi conçu :

Article 6. Les mariages ne pourront être contractés que de blancs à blancs, et de gens de couleur à gens de couleur.

Art. 7. La reconnaissance des enfants naturels ne pourra être faite que d'un père ou d'une mère blanc, en la personne d'un enfant blanc, ou d'un père ou d'une mère de couleur, en faveur d'un enfant de couleur.

Art. 8. L'adoption ne pourra également avoir lieu qu'entre individus de la même couleur.

Art. 9. Il en sera de même pour la tutelle officieuse, qui sans attribuer aucun des effets de l'adoption, en est cependant l'auxiliaire.

Art. 10. . . . .

Art. 11. . . . .

Art. 12. Toute donation entre vifs, ou simple donation, tout legs universel ou particulier, faits par un blanc à un individu de couleur, sont déclarés nuls et de nul effet.

Art. 13. . . . .

Telles sont les lois iniques qui ont régi les hommes de couleur jusqu'à ce jour.

Cette ordonnance a été mise en vigueur par M. de Laussat ; elle fut précédée et suivie d'un nombre infini d'arrêtés et de réglements. Toutes ces lois furent la base éternelle sur laquelle on posa le sanctuaire de Thémis, lieu qui aurait dû être sacré à toute influence étrangère, mais que les passions des hommes ont défiguré ! Les hommes de couleur ont été victimes et le sont encore des tristes effets qui ont pris naissance dans l'application de ces arrêtés et réglements, quoiqu'il y a une différence matérielle entre ce pays et les autres possessions françaises.

Abordons la question du cens électoral.

La position de cette colonie est déplorable : dénuée de res-sources, elle ne peut que marcher graduellement à sa ruine. Elle se ressentira long-temps et peut-être toujours des effets de la réduction opérée en 1820, sur le taux de la monnaie coloniale. C'est à cette fausse mesure financière, de M. de Laussat, qu'on doit le malaise général qui afflige cette colonie.

En effet, si l'on calculait à présent les revenus de la Guiane française, on serait bien étonné de voir que la somme de ses importations excède celle de ses exportations, d'où il résulte une balance au préjudice de la colonie au lieu d'être en sa faveur; conséquemment, elle est à charge à la métro-pole : il est constant, que plus de trois millions de dettes grèvent les propriétés. Les colons sont devenus les vrais jouets du caprice des négociants métropolitains, qui avaient faci-lité l'introduction des nègres. On les voit avec peine traînés devant les tribunaux, par les mandataires de ces négociants, pour les forcer au paiement de leurs obligations échues. Les juges, dans cette hypothèse, ne peuvent que se déterminer à l'indulgence : on accorde jusqu'à six et dix ans de délai. Ici, c'est la moindre partie de la plaie qui est mise au jour. Que l'on juge maintenant. Qui le croira !... c'est sur cette colo-nie qu'on veut établir un énorme cens électoral de 300 francs, lorsqu'en France il est fixé à 200[*]. Ne serait-on pas ridicule de poser une comparaison entre ces deux pays ? D'ailleurs on aperçoit facilement que le but de ce moyen si bien mé-dité, était d'éloigner totalement les hommes de couleur du conseil colonial. A Cayenne, il faut le dire, le moyen d'é-tablir les colléges électoraux par arrondissements, comme cela se fait en France, est impraticable dans l'intérêt général; car

[*] Dans une brochure intitulée *Projet de loi sur le régime législatif des Colonies*, nous avons vu que le cens électoral a été porté à 300 francs, sur la demande du délégué de la classe privilégiée de la Guiane fran-çaise.

il est notoirement prouvé qu'il existe actuellement dans chaque quartier plus de planteurs blancs que de personnes de couleur : l'impossibilité est donc palpable, pour qu'en faveur de ces derniers on obtienne une majorité. Le conseil colonial ne sera ainsi composé que de blancs, de là naîtront les priviléges. Si de pareils principes étaient adoptés, mieux vaudrait dire aux hommes de couleur, vous ne devez nullement participer aux bienfaits de la régénération qui s'est opérée.

Basés sur ces considérations morales, les hommes de couleur présentent à la sollicitude des législateurs, les trois moyens suivants, entre lesquels ils leur prient de faire choix, pour fixer la composition du conseil colonial à la Guiane française.

PREMIER MOYEN.

Que le cens électoral soit porté à 100 francs d'impositions directes, et le cens d'éligibilité à 200 francs ; que les impôts soient basés sur les maisons de ville, les esclaves de journées et ouvriers journaliers, et sur les patentes de première et deuxième classe ; que le planteur qui recense quinze noirs soit électeur de droit, que celui qui en recense vingt-six au moins puisse être éligible.

SECOND MOYEN.

De fixer par une estimation qui doit être faite, que l'individu qui possède en ville, une valeur réelle de 60,000 francs, est électeur de droit ; que le choix des membres au conseil colonial ne peut avoir lieu que parmi ceux qui présentent une valeur de 80,000 francs en propriété de ville.

TROISIÈME MOYEN,
PAR LEQUEL ON PEUT ÉVITER TOUTE INJUSTICE.

D'établir que le conseil colonial dans toutes les possessions françaises d'outre-mer, sera composé à moitié d'hommes pris dans les plus imposés des deux classes libres.

Ce dernier moyen nous semble être propre à trancher toute la question ; il détruira les ressorts qu'on ne cesse de faire jouer, dans le but d'entraver les hommes de couleur ; et les colonies verraient avec reconnaissance adopter une législation qui, opérant la fusion de deux classes, ferait le bonheur de cette portion de Français qui font également partie du corps social.

C'est en agissant ainsi que l'on évite les demi-mesures qui sont quelquefois funestes, lorsqu'on veut baser une législation sur des principes mal combinés.

Bien que dans le premier moyen, nous ayons indiqué les esclaves sur lesquels on peut fixer le cens électoral, cependant nous sommes forcés de l'avouer, notre conscience crie d'avance contre une base qui, si elle était adoptée, ôterait toute espérance à la classe noire de voir dans un avenir prochain, briller pour elle une aurore de liberté. Que l'on crie avec raison contre le trafic odieux de la traite des noirs ! Il est vrai qu'en 1793 la convention en décréta l'abolition ; les Anglais, également dès cette époque, avaient cherché le moyen d'anéantir un commerce réprouvé par la morale et la religion ; mais la cupidité de concert avec l'inhumanité foulèrent aux pieds cette loi et toutes celles qui l'ont suivie jusqu'à ce jour : on ne continua pas moins à faire clandestinement ce trafic jusqu'en 1829, car l'introduction n'a cessé à Cayenne que vers la fin de cette année.

On doit prendre des mesures sages pour faire disparaître les entraves que l'autorité locale met aux actes d'affranchissement*.

On établit aussi une distinction entre les anciens libres et les nouveaux affranchis qui n'ont pas atteint dix ans de jouissance des droits civils, pour participer à la jouissance des droits politiques.

---

* La république de Colombie a proclamé, il y a quelque temps, l'affranchissement graduel des esclaves : ceux qui sont actuellement dans cette position y restent, mais leur postérité naîtra libre. Ne peut-on pas, dans l'intérêt de l'humanité, suivre cet exemple ?

Ceci serait une conséquence nécessaire si l'on réduisait à six années; car nous sommes forcés de l'avouer, les droits politiques supposent des conditions de capacité, qu'un nouvel affranchi ne remplit pas.

Ma tâche est finie. Plaise à Dieu, pour les intérêts de la colonie, que les principes que j'ai indiqués soient adoptés !

O vous, honorables députés, daignez prêter l'oreille à notre voix plaintive.

Le peuple Français, en vous confiant ses hautes destinées, se reposa sur vous du soin de les accomplir : songez que, nous aussi, nous sommes Français, quoique séparés de vous par un espace de 1800 lieues. Vous avez à combattre une coterie anti-sociale, anti-française, qui conspire contre l'intelligence humaine et qui refuse à des hommes libres les droits de la liberté. Mais vous la soumettrez, elle n'est forte et ne se soutient qu'autant qu'elle trouve un appui dans les lois qui l'ont maintenue jusqu'à ce jour.

Pleins de confiance dans votre haute sagesse, nous osons espérer que vous prendrez notre demande en considération : et vous rendrez par là le bonheur à cette population, qui est depuis longues années l'objet d'une constante sollicitude.

F.-F. Le Vbloud,

Créole de Cayenne.